CW01666540

The Backpacker's Handbook

The Backpacker's Handbook

DERRICK BOOTH

Photographs by Robin Adshead

CHARLES LETTS · LONDON

© Derrick Booth 1972 and 1979
First published in Great Britain 1972

Reprinted 1975 by
Charles Letts & Company Limited
Diary House
Borough Road
London SE1 1DW

New Edition 1979, Reprinted 1980

ISBN 0 85097 382 1

For Tordis
Who showed me Norway
and much more

Cover design: Ed Perera

Printed in Great Britain by
Clarke, Doble & Brendon Ltd.
Plymouth and London

Contents

Illustrations

Preface to the Second Edition

Five eventful years span the period from when this book was first published to the revisions for this second edition. During that time backpacking has transformed hiking and lightweight camping in Britain; technology has produced some fascinating solutions to the backpacker's problems; my own fortunes have suffered some violent changes and my ideas on backpacking have matured with experience.

Yet in the main, the techniques and practices I set down in 1971 remain unaltered, and it is for this reason the architecture of Backpacker's Handbook remains familiar. In those five years I have been to the North Slope of Alaska in temperatures I had not experienced before and I have tramped through deserts with the mercury standing at levels well above blood heat and survived to remember the experience with pleasure. What I wrote at secondhand about physiology needs no revision in light of actual experience.

Nor do my ideas about techniques for camping, surviving, moving around with map and compass, single-station weather-forecasting and doing one's own thing, need any radical changes in light of my experiences in the Iranian desert, the tundra, the Peak District in winter, the Sonoran desert in summer, the rain forests of Malaysia and the crackling dry heat of Mexico—all of which have been made possible by my job and a network of friends that backpacking has brought me.

What has changed considerably is the equipment and the amount that one can buy for £1.00. When I began to write, the packframe was viewed with suspicion except by a few visionaries. The tent was a shelter that still showed its descent from the half-patrol ridge; and nobody would have guessed that man could produce fibres that almost equalled in insulation value the down of the goose and the duck, and produced sleeping bags the old campaigners would have fought over.

I do not intend to give you a new catalogue of equipment in this edition. I fell into that trap the last time and within a year many pieces had disappeared to be replaced by others of different names and specifications. Prices changed monthly as backpacking seized the imagination of thousands of people locked up in urban areas; new manufacturers grew up to cater for the expanding market and older ones merged to stand the hot blast of competition.

This new edition remains a guide only, for it is technique not equipment that makes a backpacker of you. It is still just as exciting to roam with only a bivvy bag and a home-made pack as it was in 1971, and buying the latest sophisticated design in packframe and tent will only make things a little easier in extreme conditions without actually adding anything to the special pleasure of roaming freely for days and never once having to rely on shelter and food provided by others. Believe me, the view from the top of Mount McKinley is the same whether you get to the summit by helicopter or you scramble up in gym-shoes.

I can tell you with authority that during the last five years nobody has invented the 'ideal' tent—nor will they ever. Boots still cause blisters if improperly fitted whether they are built from leather or plastics. Water still weighs about ten pounds a gallon, and you cannot do without it. Hypothermia still kills the unprepared.

I have been greatly impressed by the many readers of Backpacker's Handbook who have written to me since it first appeared. For a time I tried to overcome my need to walk alone and share the trail with others who had enthusiastically adopted the pastime after reading my book. But slowly I reverted to type, doing my own thing and learning by pragmatism. I am quite sure that had I been with others I might have been tempted to press on and I would have missed watching the American bald eagle fishing, discovering a spooky mine-shaft in the Superstition Mountains, seeing the black camel herd in Lar, the hoopoes courting in Spain and hundreds of other impressions seen through the luxury of being a solitary traveller. I ask forgiveness from all those who have sought my company and been given a refusal.

However, my solitariness must not be construed as exclusivity. I want everyone to enjoy backpacking, whether alone or in company of others. Backpacking is a way of life and spills over into other activities. Backpacking is the ultimate passport to escapism and I make no excuses for having happily revised this book for another edition.

Preface

A word in your ear

Time was when the world was limitless. Time was when the human race moved around—if at all—on its two feet. Time was when man didn't crave freedom to wander but took it for granted. A freedom unfettered by time-tables, passports, airport check-ins, organized campsites, bank holidays, early closing days, school terms and whatever.

So what did he do?

He herded together for protection. Got himself organized. He equated material possessions with successful living. He conceded his nous for the printed word on a packet or in a guide book. He lived vicariously through the flickering image on the end of a television tube. Followed the herd to the overcrowded places someone, somewhere had labelled beautiful and glimpsed the battered vista through the windscreen of his car.

And all the time man bred. So that there was hardly enough breathing space left to call beautiful anymore.

Now the wheel is going full circle. The affluent have found no satisfaction and the poor are relearning skills they discarded when they became enfranchised to materialism.

Look to the roadside and witness the well-educated young travelling like tinkers of a century ago. Follow the well-heeled to the mountains one weekend and see them engrossed in the esoteric pleasure of a mind set free in wide blue space. Go down to the canal lock-gate and keep a sharp look out for a 'middle-aged' couple launching their canoe to paddle quietly beyond the bend where the willow tree draws a curtain between the 'organized' and the 'free'.

Deep down in our souls there still lurk primeval genes which have not yet suffered the full mutation of civilizing. In some there are more freedom-seeking genes than in others. Every now and then these unique bio-chemicals get free into the system and play havoc with the rationale which tethers our everyday living, working and struggling with the noise and stink we have made for ourselves—summer Friday afternoons are a very vulnerable time for such an attack.

And the upshot is, among old and young alike, that there is now a burning urge to 'do your own thing'. To roam where the lark rises and unpolluted water thunders in cascades. To draw deep breath on the heather-scented wind which fidgets the falcon's wingtips before it stoops.

But how? How can we follow this primitive urge? Can we embrace some magic and work the trick for ourselves? Will we be able to cope after so many years of falling blindly in step behind others? What will happen to our stylized urbanity in the crudity of living simply—will it re-assert itself and so spoil the Friday afternoon day dream?

My belief is that each of us have the latent ability to live in and enjoy the outdoors in close proximity if only we are shown a basic framework of simple, commonsensical and practical ideas on which we can, each for ourselves, develop our true individual freedom. If we can walk we can travel. By travelling light and using our minds instead of forever pushing buttons in the blind belief that things will happen then I am sure we shall enjoy the remaining time left to the human race before it fouls its nest irrevocably.

By doing so we might even check the continuous loss of the quality of life before the greed for quantity makes it intolerable.

But travelling light and being almost self-sufficient is a craft which has to be learned and practised. To ignore the craft and launch forth willy-nilly is courting disappointment or at worst disaster. In articles in magazines and counselling the young I have tried to demonstrate tips, accumulated ideas and experience which have been all but bred out of us over the years. From each article has followed a big post-bag of ordinary people wanting to know more. The young bring back their friends

I have presumed then that there is a need for a book which puts together a framework of one man's primary knowledge on which to build an individualistic approach to going out of doors without being lumbered with all the useless gear many camping outfitters sell as desirable. I have tried to bring together between two covers enough experience for beginners to make choices when buying capital equipment which will not be regretted after the first flush of excitement.

It is not a book to take in the packsack—more a bolthole into which to escape in the middle of the solid urban fortresses which surround us. Not a *Complete Camper* but a guide. Not yet another of those hastily prepared camping books but an honest attempt to excite as well as inform. If it is felt to be incomplete, inaccurate or impossible I humbly apologize.

Introduction
What it's all about

Going backpacking is more a state of mind than an accomplishment. A sluggish mind accepts the adman's copy and buys without thought, finding a use for the article to justify the purchase. Travelling light on the other hand means turning this attitude upside down and being ruthless. "What can I do without?" is the premise, not "What do I need?"

It is possible to cover great distances with only what is worn, perhaps a spare pair of socks, and a smile. On the other hand, a great number of people take loads of 40 or 50 pounds on their backs, cover great distances and still smile. In between lies a wide range of individualistic choice. A choice which is dictated by the duration of the journey, the climatic zone through which the journey is made, the object of the journey and personal inclinations.

There is nothing new in the concept of going light. About 70 years ago a tailor called Tom Holding used to gather cronies in the back of his shop in Maddox Street in London and after business they would discuss ways and means of carving ounces off their camping kits. After much experimentation, they devised an outfit weighing only ten pounds and it was carried in the poaching pockets of a Norfolk jacket. These stalwarts found incredulous followers all over the world, and through their zeal the Camping Club of Great Britain and Ireland was formed.

Remember that Skipper Holding, as he was fondly called, had few of the advantages of today. No super ripstop nylons, no magnesium alloys, no accelerated freeze-dried foods, no urethanes or silicones to keep the wet out, no bottled gas, only a superabundance of enthusiasm.

Enthusiasm, then, is a word which must be steeped into the personality of anyone contemplating going light. Without it, every ounce of gear will turn to lead when the travelling gets rough. Every lovingly purchased item will be cursed and bitterly resented when it fails through the lack of respect for its capability.

But with enthusiasm, even a piece of string will become a friend; a gale an exciting experience instead of a nagging nuisance; a dawn an ecstatic moment instead of just another day.

Backpacking is available to all ages and all classes of people. With age and reasonable health only the scale of accomplishment changes when compared with the vigour of youth—the satisfaction remains undiminished. A young buck with only a bed roll and the price of his next meal can cross Europe and back. After you have turned the age of 40 mere miles matter not, only the glow on Monday morning when you return to the daily grind with batteries well charged. Six miles down the road, an open fire, supper of kebabs cooked on green sticks, a star-filled sky, heavy morning dew, a pint of best bitter in an unfamiliar country pub and six miles back again is every bit as satisfying to the mature as a 200-mile hitch to a marathon pop festival, sleeping in a newspaper 'bag', cola and hamburgers for supper, lunch and breakfast and a 200-mile hitch home would be for the young.

You can either travel in solitary solace or gregarious groups according to your temperament. But a word of warning to those who have never travelled alone before. Unless you can stand your own company for days on end, without talking to another human for perhaps 10 or 15 hours, take along a friend you understand and trust. Going alone tests your personality to the full and it has to be in balance.

You must possess a mind which is either capable of flooding itself constantly with ideas to be examined or you must be possessed with a kind of mindlessness which is satisfied with a tuneless whistle, a paper-backed novel and the simple thought of what the next meal will be.

Going alone is not for those who were warned of bogeymen behind the curtain in childhood. For these people there will still be too many fears of the unknown around them—although in public they will be the last to admit it—to be at ease completely alone.

Every little noise in the night will bring a whiff of panic. Suppressed fears will bring clumsiness, and when you are alone there is little margin for error. Better to travel with a friend who accepts inconsequential chatter alternating with long periods of silence than to miss the pleasure of being out of doors through the foolishness of improper upbringing which later induces the fear of loneliness.

Travelling light is great for families. Dad becomes the big brave, the youngsters rollick along in his wake with mama squaw bringing up the rear. Dad carries the biggest load—it is evidence of his masculinity—the youngster can carry quite useful contributions and the faithful squaw has her backpack nicely adjusted to carrying goodies for her family and the essential things which make her feel still womanly.

What usually happens in our family is that my wife's chores such as cooking are taken away from her as she soaks up the sun; everyone likes to cook out of doors. Washing up is simple enough with one-pan meals and nobody minds scouring out his own dish. Fire-making and tending is men's work, so is setting up the tents. Shopping is a shared adventure in an unfamiliar village.

Sometimes my son and I go off on our own and the division of duties falls automatically between us. I can recommend father and son trips to any man who has a boy in his early teens. You get to know much more about youthful viewpoints and in the outdoors instruction from parent to sibling never sounds like preaching. Fathers, in turn, will find their methods of travelling light and attitudes to life in general criticized in a way no other relationship can match. Buying new gear for birthdays and high days is also a pleasant indulgence for any father for his son.

Talking of buying equipment, I ought to say that penny for new penny nothing quite matches travelling light as a recreational investment. Even buying the best, a good, well thought-out full kit should not cost more than a month's pay. With proper care it will last at least ten years. A few pounds a year can't be a bad buy, for not only does it bring pleasure while in use, it also invokes another kind of pleasure in the long winter months when repairs are made or improvements devised. Perhaps a new 'ideal' tent is cut out and sewn up on the kitchen table or a knife honed to perfection and oiled ready for the spring. Whatever it is, the pleasure is real.

The secret of buying lightweight equipment is to buy the very best you can afford at the time—even if it means going without that other shiny thingummyjig you have had your eye on. A top-flight piece of gear is not only a joy to own but it gives no qualms when it is put to the test in adverse conditions. A rucksack often becomes an heirloom as does a knife or compass. I have seen so many disappointments in youngsters who have saved hard and tried to outfit themselves completely on their savings, only to find that re-kitting was necessary in the same season because they bought all the wrong things. Much better to buy one good essential and put up with an improvisation or two than try to get the most with the least.

My American backpacking friend—now in his sixties—reckons adventure starts around the first firebreak from the car park. He lives in Arizona and his special reason for travelling light is to take a metal detector to the desert and the dry gulch looking for saddle harness and revolvers in the places where the West was won. My Canadian friend has a thing about canoe travel—paddling and portaging solo out in Northern Ontario. My son's friend goes solitary to wild places to read classics undisturbed. My son hunts fossils and minerals. I hunt differences in language and go abroad listening to countryside accents and dialects. The photographer who helped to illustrate this book is a wildfowler and ornithologist. My neighbour's son is a student who is trying to see as much of Europe as possible.

We all travel light for different purposes with different gear even. Only two of our little group travel light because we can't afford to travel any other way and all of us travel this way because we enjoy it. I have no hesitation in recommending it as a hobby and it could even become a way of life.

What I have written on the following pages is a very subjective view of what I have done over the years of travelling light. My selection of equipment—especially when I mention or recommend one manufacturer's article and omit to mention another's which is probably equally effective—is open to severe criticism by other travellers who have gone down the trail ahead of me and others who are tramping down behind, not to mention the manufacturers. Each of us knows best.

But all of us will agree that what we know we have acquired the hard way. There has been no standard work to guide us, only enthusiasm and some fellowship with similar minds. Which doesn't help the newcomers eager to get going next week.

And another point often overlooked by critics is this. Pressure on recreational spaces has brought codification in other sports to regulate the activity 'for the good of all'. Backpackers are a long way off codification by the very nature of their craft. Yet unless newcomers learn basic craft as soon as possible some Minister of Sport and his band of civil servants will be codifying our activity for us. So this book is intended as much as anything to help newcomers not to make expensive mistakes which will provoke authority and regulation.

Public Rights of Way exist all over Britain, thousands of miles of them. If we don't use them, the anti-freedom brigade will eventually see that they are sealed off. Travelling light should help to keep the weeds down on those pathways 'that nobody uses'.

1

Gathering the bits and pieces

Put at its lowest and simplest level, travelling light is moving around in the clothes you stand up in and a toothbrush stuck in your top pocket. Come to that, you can even eliminate the toothbrush and rub salt on your teeth with a forefinger! But travelling like this demands ultra-stoic qualities, lots of luck and a kind of drop-out mentality.

One rung up from this level can be practised pleasurably by the young with the minimum of equipment and a membership to the Youth Hostels Association. A regulation 8-ounce cotton sleeping bag is mandatory and costs little. Into a waterproof airline-style shoulder bag goes a pair of wash'n wear trousers, two pairs of underpants, one T-shirt, three pairs of socks, a polythene toilet bag with comb, toothbrush protected with aluminium foil, and paste, a J-cloth, a small cake of hotel soap, a pair of nail clippers, a small pack of Kleenex tissues, a tiny plastic pill bottle with half a dozen aspirin tablets, a piece of card with two needles embedded in it and three or four yards of thread wrapped around it together with two safety pins, a small sachet of sticking plaster dressings, a part-used tube of Savlon, a part-used tube of Flypel. Take also a 35 mm film can with snap-on plastic lid containing two boxes of windproof matches, a dessert spoon, a half-pint plastic mug, a combination can opener, crown cork lifter and corkscrew, and also a big bandana handkerchief.

Worn on the person are a pair of good walking shoes or boots, a pair of thin socks and a pair of heavier woollen socks over, a pair of hard wearing woollen trousers, a pair of underpants, a T-shirt with a light lambswool sweater over and all topped with a heavy Scotch wool mackinaw shirt provided with at least one pocket.

Around the neck on a thin nylon cord there is a whistle, in the trouser pocket there is a good carbon steel clasp knife honed to perfection and secured with another lanyard of light nylon cord to the belt. A large polythene bag in 350-gauge material doubles as a poncho and an emergency bivvy bag for that odd night out when the hostel is full and it's a long way to the next.

This list, or something like it, is the very least a person can collect to travel in reasonable comfort and economy in a temperate climate where there are hostels or cheap hotels to provide the evening's shelter and source of main meals. A breakfast the following morning before setting off to the next hostel means there is no need to collect cooking equipment, lunch being, say, an apple and piece of cheese or a snack bought on the way.

The all up weight of such an outfit would be about eight or nine pounds including the shoulder bag but not including the clothes normally worn. The drawback of the outfit is the need to find shelter and food every night. Not only does this put a strain on keeping to an itinerary but it also costs money—a budget of at least a few pounds each day, not including fares.

This is a most economical outfit and it includes a pair of boots, heavy wool shirt and knife. Most of the other items are normally owned anyway.

I have given this outfit in detail to demonstrate one simple fact—weight and its accretion to the outfit by stealth. Old timers used to reckon that every extra ounce in the pack shouldered up in the morning would feel like a pound at the end of a long gruelling tramp. I know what they meant.

Weight, then, is the enemy. It has to be mastered at every stage if it is not to master you and spoil your fun. Every doubtful gramme has to be thrown out—it will sneak back again if you don't remain vigilant.

Before you purchase any item of kit go to a fishing tackle or hardware shop and buy two spring balances. One scale should read 0–4 pounds by ounces and the other 0–25 pounds by ½-pounds, or be modern and work in kilos. They are small enough to pocket easily and should be taken on every shopping expedition.

The manufacturer's or retailer's catalogue usually lists a weight for each item. A check with your personal spring balance will usually reveal a discrepancy—on the bad side. There is nothing underhand about the vendor's sales methods—an ounce give or take to him is immaterial. To you it is vital.

Spring balances in hand we can now begin the selection and collection of an outfit which will suit you and your particular type of fun.

Firstly decide what you intend to do with your new-found hobby. Is it a means to cover as much ground as possible as cheaply as possible? Or do you plan a birdwatching trip to the edge of one of Iceland's glaciers? Do you want to potter around your local province every weekend of the summer or do you want to go to the wilderness in the UK or abroad? Overnight or a month away? Summer wandering or hardweather survival?

If you are beginning from scratch you will have to learn to walk before you can run and you may find that after three or four nights out, travelling light is not for you. Buying a pile of expensive equipment cannot guarantee success and its disposal will be difficult if you opt out for more organized pleasures after the initial failure.

Selection of equipment is a very personal thing so I will attempt to review all the gear I have personally tested and leave you with the choice to suit your need. However, there are certain basic rules. Equipment can be categorized into three divisions: essentials, utilities and luxuries. Your selection from each heading will be your own affair. But don't forget the enemy, weight, just hanging around waiting to slip in through any open zip fastener and into the deep corner of your pack.

Before you start buying send to each camping outfitter for his catalogue—addresses of the principal companies are at the back of the book. Ponder over each booklet and you will discover common items—there are not that many manufacturers of lightweight equipment. Compare what is offered against the relative merits of the items in the three categories listed above. And then do a lot of thinking. If you have a good shop handy, go and browse around and talk to the sales assistants—many of them are climbers, canoeists or campers in their spare time. Don't buy anything until you are convinced of its need.

The knack which has to be learned early when going light is the need to make one item do as many jobs as possible—although this can be taken to ridiculous limits. For instance, 'shelter' listed under

ESSENTIALS	UTILITIES	LUXURIES
Emergency shelter	Bedding	Washing bowl
Food	Tentage	Airbed
Footwear	Portable fire	Writing paper, etc.
Insulation	Cooking equipment	Reading matter
Survival items	Specialist waterproof wear	Radio
Knife	Packframe or rucksack	Swimwear
Shoulder bag	Extra clothing	Fire grid
Basic toiletries	First aid kit	Reflector oven
Salt	Alternative footwear	Foor goodies and canned goods
Passport (foreign travel)	Extra toiletries	Camera, binoculars, etc.
	Maps	Musical instruments
	Water carrier	Small saw or axe
	Cordage	

the 'Essentials' heading can be a polythene bag which once wrapped around a mattress or it can be properly made cagoule—a sort of waterproof smock. Shelter can be a true tent or a large sheet of vinyl draped over saplings or stones.

The point I am making is this: A polythene bag has to be adapted—not entirely satisfactorily—to become a tent or a poncho. And air holes have to be left in it so that you don't suffocate. A cagoule on the other hand well-made is at once temporary shelter as well as the best storm gear you can buy. It will weigh less than a large polythene bag too. A true tent is a real home—even in the worst conditions—whereas a sheet of vinyl although cheap provides only, at best, a good bivouac.

There is no such thing as the perfect kit—only the best you can afford at the time. And sure as tomorrow's dawn you will be constantly changing your kit as your hobby flowers.

Under the heading 'Essentials' I have listed the kit in some detail at the beginning of this chapter. This outfit is the cheapest, most flexible and lightest you can hope to venture far with.

So let's turn to the next heading 'Utilities'.

PACK

A proper pack becomes necessary once your load exceeds ten pounds. A pack has two functions, to carry the load as comfortably as possible and provide a rational way of separating each item from the next in some sort of order. Tidiness, you will find, is essential if you are not to temporarily lose your temper or your can opener. A pack with pockets and sub-divisions gives the lightweighter a tidy distribution of his load, and providing a set method of loading is adhered to, will keep items in a regular place for instant retrieval.

I would advise against buying ex-government packs. They are usually designed for a special purpose, are heavy and awkward to use. Soldiers under orders are a different proposition from civilians moving freely for pleasure, when it comes to pack design.

For entirely different reasons, the beloved Bergan-type framed rucksack of forty years ago is now a poor buy for lightweighters. It carries the load in an anatomically inferior way, and it weighs far too much. A pack of any sort should never weigh more than 10 per cent of the gross load—less if it can be managed. Many Bergan-type rucksacks weigh 6 pounds or more—6 pounds of dead weight.

Cotton duck takes up quite a lot of weight in water during a prolonged downpour. PU coated nylon does not.

Since the first edition of this book appeared the choice and variety of packs suitable for the full range of backpacking has widened so considerably that to make recommendations would be foolish. At the one end there are small soft packs for day hiking or big enough to carry an overnight kit in case of being stranded in the mountains; and at the other there are so many ingenious solutions to carrying heavy loads without too much discomfort. My kit box contains several packs of various ages and for various duties, and looking back over the last ten years I am amazed that manufacturers can still come up with a new idea which has some improvement over what has gone before. The final choice a newcomer must make for himself will be based on the subjective decision of what feels right.

Physiologically we are slightly different from each other, not only in height and girth, but also in the development of a number of bones on which the pack must sit when loaded. Correct adjustment of the harness of any pack will at worst improve a bad pack to make it just bearable, while the correct adjustment of a premium brand frame and pack will make hiking with a load almost a joy—I did say almost!

The best way to adjust a pack for comfort is to load it up as though you are going on a hike, strip off and stand in front of the mirror. Observe that we all have two dimples at the lower end of the back; these dimples are the surface indication of the strongest point of the human frame—the back of the pelvis. It is on this saddle that we let the main load lie. It does not flex when walking and is merely an enlarged vertibrae.

Now adjust the shoulder straps until the saddle band of the pack—whether it is a soft pack or a frame—sits squarely over the two dimples. Once you have the feel of the correct position it will be much easier to adjust when you are wearing all your clothes for cold weather.

If you find the pack will not sit properly, no matter how much you adjust it, then it is the wrong pack for you. See if there are any alternative anchor points for the straps and the saddle. If not, get rid of it, for it will cause you nothing but bother. If by adjusting the position of the strap anchors you can bring the load

Figure 1. *Putting the vectors to work*. This illustrates why the packframe and sack is the best medium to heavy load carrier (Cunningham)

directly over the broad part of the pelvis you will find greater comfort.

What now has to be decided is how well the pack is built to distribute the load evenly over this strong point of the back, and whether the shoulder straps are wide and padded enough to prevent chafing, lumpiness, breathlessness, swinging, and general fatigue due to the mechanics of pack design.

No matter how well a soft pack is designed it cannot begin to compare with the properly made lightweight frame. But before discussing packframes, let me tell you about a mad idea I once had for ultra-lightweighting. I looked at those two dimples and wondered if one could fly against convention by hanging the pack downwards instead of building it up over the shoulders.

I persuaded an American packframe firm I knew well to build me what amounted to a big pouch to which was sewn a broad webbing belt as a waist harness to strap it to my body. The pouch had lugs sewn on the top through which light straps could be threaded. The pouch was opened from either end by a zipper and there was a smaller inner-pouch elasticated at the top.

I found I could stow most essential things in the pouch such as basic food, extra socks, a small collapsable gas stove and a light wool sweater. Once this was packed firmly I could roll a short piece of insulating foam around my lightweight summer sleeping-bag and lash it on top with straps through the two lugs. On one hip threaded over the waist strap I carried an insulated campaigner's water-bottle and on the other I threaded my stainless steel Sierra cup (an American symbol of packing, with a shallow pan and a wire bail hooked to hold and thread under the belt) and then I had a small nylon pouch threaded on the front to hold spare film, flash gun and camera stuff; while on the other side by the buckle was another clipover pouch which contained goodies to nibble at on the trail.

The trousers were made with two front thigh pockets; one held the map and the other held a most useful cape I have with hood and draw string skirt that doubles as a bivouac. Shirt pockets completed all my stowage of bits and bobs—I have never walked so freely in my life and had enough gear to last for two or three nights out in summer conditions. So you see, a pack *is* essential but it need not be so big as to beg to be filled with all sorts of stuff you really don't need. Because before you are even aware of it, you have a 30-pound load on your shoulders and misery with every step.

For winter travel and extended hiking in wildernesses I believe there is no other carrier to beat the big packframe and sack. This highly developed piece of kit originated in the United States and if you will look to figure 1 you will see the mechanics of pack-frame-wearing and the advantages which follow their use. Pack-frames come into their own when loads exceed 15 pounds and they can go on carrying loads up to 100 pounds with some degree of comfort—although anything beyond 35 pounds is beyond the scope of this book.

The disadvantage of the packframe is its uncompromising angularity and rigidity when off the back. Packframes are not easy to get in and out of cars; do not make for good bedfellows in tiny tents; and are a nuisance in crowds and busy trains. They are also vulnerable to theft from behind in busy bazaars and crowded tourist spots. Airlines just love chucking them on and off the baggage carts to see if they will break, and customs officers always think you are carrying 15 pounds of cannabis resin inside them when you pass through and insist on a complete strip search. In sub-tropics and really hot countries a packframe can be unbearably hot and costs are high too.

Nevertheless, I am a confirmed backpacker. The advantage of carrying a load on a pelvic girdle and shoulder straps or changes of each from time to time far outweighs the disadvantages when used in temperate zones and wildernesses.

But there are pitfalls to watch for from the ever-growing range of these contraptions. Firstly the frame must be really rigid and preferably with joints that are shielded—arc welded rather than brazed—although I will allow there are things to be said for joints made from compression fittings that screw up providing you can really tighten up those cross-headed screws on the trail. Many frames, despite the beautifully anodized colours, are made from soft aluminium alloy. Consequently they bend under load. Try bending the frame in the shop—when the assistant is not looking—and set aside all those frames that give under your muscle power. Set aside too, all those frames that have a top cross-bar high up—you won't be able to crane your head back to see up to where you are climbing. The best frames have a V-bar at the top to allow the head to lean back without banging the frame.

Look to the method of attaching the bag too. Clevis pins and split rings seem a good idea but try removing a snow-covered bag to take in the tent with frozen fingers and you will understand what I mean. Loops are too loose and spring clips do get lost. But I prefer spring clips and carry a few spares.

The choice of bag is yours. The objective is to get the heaviest part of the load as high as possible and this will decide where you are going to stow your sleeping-bag and insulating pad—like underneath! Make sure the bag is polyurethane coated nylon and double stitched. Zippers should be large and plastic to prevent freezing, and all covered by flies. Friction toggles make closing the shawl cover a lot easier than lashings. But remember, no pack is waterproof, even if it is made from truly waterproof material. Every pass of the sewing machine needle makes a hole and through the hole comes rain. Now you can buy a waterproof cover to fit over the pack or you can wrap all your gear in polybags sold for home freezer fiends. I prefer the latter, but the cape I was mentioning earlier does have a huge camel hump formed in it and I can wear the cape right over everything, pack and all.

Adjusting the packframe along the lines I suggested earlier is most important. Too often I have seen women and youngsters wearing a packframe far too big for them and the saddle webbing actually hanging under the derrière! So make sure your packframe has a wide waist harness which you can cinch up really firmly at the front. Get the buckle down as low on the abdomen as possible so that the sides of the belt are passing actually over the hip bone of the pelvis and not above it. If it is done properly the packframe becomes part of you and you can stride out and swing the arms freely to get the push and rhythm of walking properly, and well.

One thing that gets on my nerves is a pack that tinkles and jangles as I walk because loose metal bits dangle about. A good friendly squeak of the harness is one thing but a tinkle, jingle, tap-tap, ringle is maddening when the going is hard and you are tired. There is another annoying habit with packframes that is easily cured. These awkward frames have a nasty habit of sliding down on the floor when leaned against something. Try putting orthopaedic walking-stick caps on the bottom ends and your sliding troubles are over.

The packframe and the tent are two of the largest and most expensive bits of kit you will be required to buy. My advice is don't buy either to begin with until you have looked around carefully—borrow different styles if you can. And finally, when you are convinced of your needs, buy wisely. A cheap buy—usually a pack copied from a top-range model by a sweat shop in Korea or Taiwan—is so inferior to the real thing that you will soon come to realize how you wasted your money. There is no substitute for quality when buying anything to do with backpacking, and this is especially true of packframes and sacks.

FOOTWEAR

Your feet are your vehicle when it comes to travelling light. Even the hitch-hiker must be prepared to walk many miles as he meanders down his unplanned trail, and the wilderness walker who goes lame could be in danger.

Two conditions must be fulfilled. A high standard of foot hygiene and properly fitted boots for those who will be carrying an extra stone or more on their backs for journeys in excess of ten miles a day. I will discuss foot hygiene later, but when it comes to boots I cannot help you more than suggest you go to a good class camp outfitter with a mountain shop and put yourself in the boot fitter's hands so to speak. Tell him a price—be prepared to pay £8 upwards—and be guided by what he says.

A few points to bear in mind. Nothing in a backpacker's inventory is more important than his boots. Some of the points to look for in a medium-priced boot are shown in figure 2. A proper fit should be obtained at the hands of a good boot fitter—ordering boots by post is courting disaster. If you weigh more than 10 stone you will need ½-inch wearing soles, one or two subsoles or midsoles of stiff leather together with a leather insole. Otherwise you will feel the trail through the soles of your feet and they will soon tire. The heel counter and toe cap should be hardened internally to give support and protection, and toes should be able to move freely when the boot is laced up. Soles should be nicely rounded to give spring to your stride. If the soles are too flat and stiff and your heel rises more than about ⅛ inch with each step you will have blisters. Proprietary soles have moulded cleats designed in such a way that any tendency to slide on ball-bearing-like stones is checked. Grip is improved on rough surfaces and sharp pointed stones cannot be felt through the soles.

Vibrams or Kletters give confidence and absorb some of the hammer the road can give to your feet. But watch out when moving over wet grass or moss—they can slide without warning.

The best boots for hard use come from Austria and Italy, with the German boots marching close behind. Czechoslovakia also makes some good boots at a reasonable price, while the Poles satisfy the cheaper end of the market.

Britain's well-known bootmaker, Hawkins of Northampton, has a wide range of well-made, reasonably priced boots. My own are a Hawkins Pinnacle fell boot and I have no complaint after many hundreds of miles.

Two words of warning: don't buy cheap 'Spanish fell boots — they are useless. Made from canvas-backed cheap suède on moulded soles, often formed from reclaimed automobile tyres, they will fall apart in days and soak your feet in sweat and rain in the meantime.

Secondly, don't try to dry boots out by putting them close to a fire—you will ruin them and eventually your feet too. Stuff newspaper inside to soak up the worst and then air them thoroughly

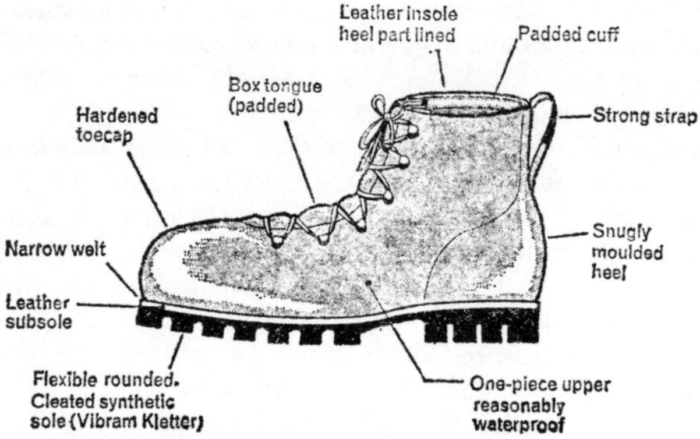

Figure 2. *The backpacker's vehicle*

until dry. Too much dubbin will rot the stitching, so after they have been well run in, brush over with shoe polish from time to time and restrict the dubbin or boot oil to two or three times in the season.

Never venture forth on a long trip without breaking your boots in to the shape of your foot. Walk round the neighbourhood when you first buy them and then increase your mileage gradually until after a month you can wear them all day without fatigue. Give your boots a chance and they will become trusted friends—ignore them and they will play hell with your feet and spoil your fun.

There is a cheaper alternative to top grade boots for those simply experimenting with lightweight travel. Go to a shop specializing in industrial boots and shoes. Look over the stock and get a fitting. This footwear is high-grade and yet can cost considerably less than specialist boots lasted abroad. What you wear does not matter half so much as comfort and safety they can bring in out of the way places.

Shun all plastics except as wearing soles. Plastics cannot 'breathe' to rid your foot of sweat and you will suffer—especially in cold weather.

Some people travelling light make do with boots throughout the journey. But I prefer to have an alternative despite the extra weight penalty. Second-line shoes can be as simple as a sculptured wooden platform, 'flip-flops' made in Hong Kong, sandals, tennis shoes or moccasins.

I use soled moccasins—genuine Canadian raw-hide, thong-tied moccasins. They weigh under one pound, dry super soft even after being soaked in morning dew, and slip on like gloves.

Remember that if you choose tennis shoes they are made from a high proportion of rubber, which not only promotes foot sweating but also weighs several ounces more than leather.

SHELTER

Shelter has but one prime function, to prevent you becoming exposed. The wind-chill scale shown in figure 21 illustrates how the body can lose heat rapidly without warning. Even the thinnest membrane between you and the wind is efficient at decreasing the the risk of exposure. If it is waterproof as well it can prevent a soaking. Polythene sheeting fulfils this simple requirement for shelter. A polythene bag big enough to cover the entire body is the fell walker and mountain man's first line of defence when caught out in the open.

Travellers going light can put a polythene bag to use as a shelter, but it is not ideal because every ounce of moisture given off by the body in its regular action of maintaining a heat balance will condense on the inside of the bag and soak back into your clothing. Another danger with a polythene bag is static electricity which causes it to adhere to skin and clothing and could lead to suffocation.

A polythene bag can be improved with springy green sticks cut to size to make hoops inside. And the packframe jammed across the mouth after you are inside gives adequate air space without loss of protection from the elements.

One step up from the polythene bivvy bag is a 'tarp' made from ¾-ounce urethane-coated nylon measuring about 8 feet by 10 to which has been sewn a number of nylon webbing loops in as many ways as suits the owner. The tarp can then be draped over a wall or cycle, slung from a tree, wrapped around a wearer, turned into an opened tent according to the extent of the camper's imagination. I used to carry one of these sheets, weighing about 1¾ pounds, and found it very useful. Most good outfitters sell them or you can buy the urethane-coated nylon and run one up for yourself. It folds up to very small bulk. Choose a light colour though—orange preferably—

nothing is worse than holing up under a gloomy coloured tarp all day in driving rain.

When we come to true tents the choice widens and careful selection is necessary. To my mind any tent intended for one or two adults weighing more than 3½ pounds is too heavy. You will see well-known outfitters offering 'lightweight' tents weighing 10 pounds or more and begin to wonder if Skipper Holding ever existed!

A lightweight tent must fulfil several functions: Be weather-tight, windproof, accommodate one or two persons in reasonable comfort, remain snug and dry in bad weather, have good aerodynamic properties, have protection from insects and standing water, reasonable headroom and a psychologically acceptable colour. A good tent should be so simple to erect that it can be done in the dark with a Force 8 gale blowing. When packed its bulk must not be more than a lump measuring about nine inches in diameter by twelve inches long. Poles and pegs must be light and strong without excessive bulk.

Nylon has made great inroads into tent making. Fine linen lawn used to be the best material for super-lightweights, but ripstop, urethane-coated nylon, has it beaten hands down except on one important point. Urethane-covered nylon is impervious which means it will suffer from the same condensation drawback as polythene.

Tent makers have used several ingenious solutions to get round this penalty. Some incorporate cotton panels, others make coated flysheets and openweave, silicone-coated inners. Others tackle condensation by preventing its formation.

Condensation forms when the temperature of moisture-laden air is suddenly reduced. A chilled membrane of nylon is perfect for forming condensation. But by incorporating a thin layer of insulating foam (and raising the skin temperature) condensation can be prevented from forming.

Looking around the choices available to the light traveller inside my arbitrary barrier of 3½ pounds I have found three true tents which meet nearly all of the specifications listed above—there is no such thing as the ideal tent. Just outside the barrier at around four or five pounds are two more. Choosing a tent is just about like choosing a wife. All have their good points and their bad, but it is only when you have been living with your tent for a long time under adverse conditions can you be assured of a faith-

The invitation to walk an empty trail is the irresistible urge for any backpacker

When you climb higher and higher the world becomes your own, just so long as you have the right gear to survive . . .

ful friend for life. The shelves of the outfitters are stuffed with tents of all shapes and duties, colours and materials. Some are single-skin; others have two. Some have nesting poles; others have silly bits of aluminium that fall apart as you are trying to set them up. Some have meat-skewers for pegs; others have heavy steel angle irons. The problem for a newcomer is knowing where to start.

Ideally, the better outfitter will have a range of lightweight tents set up in his showroom for you to crawl around in and lying there on your back you can get some idea of the space, a good idea of the workmanship and a great feeling of adventure. Be careful of this last emotion. Remember what I said about wives and tents or otherwise you will be seduced as you lie there in the warm showroom, and will whip out your cheque book and be stuck with a bitch of a thing. Be calm and canny.

Firstly, how easy was it to get inside? Did you trip over a valance, collapse the tent pole or catch your neck on the main guy? Yes? Then think how this will be in the wilds with a layer of snow on the ground or the wind howling like a soundtrack from Macbeth. If it was easy enough, examine why. I believe that the smaller the tent the more necessary it is to have A-poles at the entrance. If the tent is to be shared with others, the A-pole allows somebody to get out or in without you getting a boot in your face as you sleep. A-poles are more stable. A-poles are heavier.

Now look at the top of the pole—if you are viewing a tent with two skins—and see how the manufacturer makes his separation between inner tent and fly. This feature is essential in order to achieve a good set and eliminating condensation. The better tents have a well-engineered extension of the pole to give at least a four inch minimum separation all round. Hanging a loop over the spike with a metal eye ensures the inner tent cannot do anything but slop around even if the fly is set right. Much better for the inner tent to have a proper grommet at both ends of the ridge through which the main pole spike passes and on which two small extension pieces provide the spikes for the fly.

On any tent you might buy that has both an inner and a fly, pull it from the bag and put the grommet hole of the inner against the grommet hole of the fly and then asking the assistant to thread these two on a ball-point pen or something; draw the two tents out with even tension and see where the other two grommets lie.

Unless they come together and there is no sag of one of the pieces of material, the tent will never set properly. It is amazing how many manufacturers—even the top names—never seem to pay enough attention to this essential detail of dimensional accuracy.

Now anything not rigid that is supported between two points will hang in a natural catenary curve. Only those tents with ridge poles will ever set so well that both the ridge of the inner tent and the fly are perfectly straight lines. Some good manufacturers are aware of this natural law and cut their designs with a catenary curve already in the stitching of the ridge. Full marks. But did they go on to make the seam waterproof? Examine closely, for unlike cotton, nylon does not swell when wet and the needle holes make a fine showerbath in heavy rain.

The same goes for the floor too. Unless the seam where the cloth is joined is properly waterproofed, standing water will leach up through it and soak your kit. Better to have a full tank floor where the sides come right up a few inches and the corners, where the peg loops are attached, must be doped to make them waterproof too. Now we have a flexible tray around which the rest of the tent can be built.

When nylons first came in manufacturers merely did a straight substitution from cotton and ran into all sorts of troubles. Most of these troubles have now been ironed out among the better companies but imported tents from the Far East are still perpetuating the errors, because it saves money. Beware!

Zippers should be heavy duty plastic to prevent freeze-ups, although flyscreen doors can be lightweight coiled-tooth self-repairing nylon. Remember if you see Velcro fastenings, they relax under load and get thoroughly tangled up with flyscreen material. Good as it is, I leave Velcro alone when it comes to tents.

Run your fingers down every seam to be seen. Was it made with a double needle machine so the two runs of machining are parallel? If not, try and see if the run and fell of the join is actually connected to material all the way—look against the light to see this. Loose frayed bits sticking through the seam are a dead give-away of poor machining and even poorer quality control inspection.

Are all the main guyed seams sewn with a tape on the inside so that all stresses are taken on the tape and not on the material? Discard all those that overlook this point. A seam must withstand enormous stresses in exposed conditions and omitting tape is penny pinching which could cause trouble.

Now open up the peg bag and see what sort of tackle the manufacturer has given you to secure your precious tent. Meat-skewers are a sign of a manufacturer that cares more about sales than product after-service—and certainly one that has never taken his products out for full field trials. Hook pegs are prettty useless too for the guy can slip up and loosen in the hook. Ring heads are better, but aluminium angle pegs found on Scandinavian tents are about the best all-rounders. They have enormous holding power without too much penetration and if they bend they can be straightened fairly easily. They have a hole near the top for pulling them out too. The manufacturer that offers smaller pegs for the ground cloth and stouter ones for the main spread has obviously thought about his product and the overall weight.

Now examine the guylines. The manufacturer who ties up bits of nylon codline with useless tiny aluminium runners with the loop to the ground hasn't done his homework. But if you see lines made up with a small loop from a bowline at the peg end and the runner loop set to the tent you can be assured the maker has some practical experience. I always remove aluminium sliders—they slip and chafe if tucked back into the slot—and tie Tarbucks instead (*see page* 154) and I never trust any guyline knot tied by a manufacturer. Some years go I used to visit a reputable manufacturer's plant from time to time and the women in the guy-tying department used to ask me for lessons on how to tie a bowline—the securest loop you can tie. A few weeks later I'd be doing the same lesson all over again and to the same people, so much for manufacturer's knots!

Now rustle the fabric of the inner and the outer tent. Does it make a noise like starched tissue? Can you imagine the noise this will make in a high wind? Go for the softer coatings if you sleep lightly, and watch out for acrylic coatings, they chafe off. Run a finger-nail down the inside of the fabric on which the coating has been applied and if there is no white mark, then it is certainly not acrylic and most probably polyurethane.

I believe the best guide to a manufacturer's consciousness about his product lies in the shape and style of the stuff bag. We are soon aware that poles are a damned nuisance and are then carried vertically in the pack for easy access, but if the stuff bag is long and sausage shaped, how are we going to carry it easily? Almost any lightweight one/two-man tent will stow in a bag six inches in diameter and ten inches long. That sort of shape will lash easily on top of the pack under the shawl top and be the first object you find when you stop for the night halt. Not only that, it will never snag in tall undergrowth as you battle your way through. Nothing is more fatiguing than being thrown off balance by an overhanging pack. Be like the cat—if your whiskers can get through a hole, so can you.

The final touch of quality is a small nylon drawstring bag for pegs. I mark the outside of the bag with a chinagraph crayon to tell me how many pegs I should have when I've struck camp. It makes you look around carefully if those in the hand don't tally —saves tears at night too.

WATERPROOF CLOTHING

Not all your lightweight days will be sunny—on the other hand they will not always be wet either. So it is necessary to buy storm clothing which is completely waterproof yet as light as possible to add as little as practicable to the total burden when not being worn.

The cagoule—a kind of rain smock with a hood and drawstring bottom—is the most satisfactory main garment and waterproof leggings or trousers worn under the cagoule and over the trousers or slacks complete the waterproof envelope.

Cagoules come in many colours and each have different refinements. But look for the quality of stitching and the method by which the maker waterproofs his seams. These two points will give you a good clue to the garment's reliability when it comes to long use in hard weather.

A cagoule and leggings can be made at home for about a third of the cost.

A backpacker's cagoule should weigh about 8 or 9 ounces, have double elasticated cuffs, a box tongue to the neck which draws up with the hood string, a one-piece yoke, and a drawstring bottom. Vents to the back and armholes, zippers over the trouser pockets and cold temperature toggles on the drawstrings. All these refinements are to be found on the better garments.

Choice of colour is personal, but bear in mind the use to which you will put your lightweight travelling. For bird watching or natural history work, choose forest green. For mountain and fell walking, choose royal blue or orange. Hitch-hiking, choose orange or yellow for maximum eye-catching.

The leggings can be made at home from PU-coated nylon material or bought from better class outfitters. I prefer leggings to overtrousers because they vent the crotch area. The legs of any overtrouser should be wide enough to be slipped on over boots and then either drawn up by elastic or a snap fastener at the ankle. An instep tape to prevent them rising with each stride is a further desirable feature.

Leggings can also be worn when walking through heather and scrub country to prevent the snagging of trousers. Early morning walking through bracken country, overgrown railway tracks or long marshland grass is made much more pleasurable with waterproof leggings.

The cagoule and leggings together form the first line of bad-weather defence in a lightweighter's outfit. A true lightweighter walking between hostels and bothies can rely on his cagoule and overtrousers as an emergency bivouac if he is caught out without proper shelter.

Even so, any PU nylon cagoule and overtrouser will cause condensation to form on the inside from body moisture trying to find its way to the air. Better to choose a slightly larger cagoule than a tailored fit and the bottom should always be left free to allow good air circulation unless you are descending a hill which causes updraughts. Then draw the skirt up to waist high with the drawstring.

A cagoule will cost about £6 and leggings about £1 if made up at home. Together they should weigh no more than one pound. With reasonable care they should last several seasons, although continual chafing of shoulder straps will cause the PU coating to deteriorate. There is no satisfactory method of reproofing woven nylon.

Cagoules provide good weather protection but the nylon material has a rather 'unfriendly' feel about it. When the hood is up there is a tendency for the space behind the neck to feel chilly and draughty. I recommend you buy a big cotton bandanna—a 27-inch square of a colour to suit your fancy. This bandanna can be used for several other things—a scarf, head cap in your sleeping bag on a cold night, dust shield for the face in open country, sling for injured arms or hands, and even a towel, so it is worth its weight in your kit allowance. When wearing a cagoule, wear the bandanna as a neck scarf to seal off the gap in the nape. Cagoules can also be worn as protection against penetrating cold winds.

SLEEPING BAGS

Your choice of sleeping bag depends so much upon what you want to do with your new-found hobby of backpacking. Travel from hostel to hostel demands only the standard YHA cotton bag. But this has no insulation value for sleeping out of doors or in barns and bothies.

Cold-weather camping in winter or journeys to northern climates in summer demands high quality goose down bags. Jaunts to hot climates or countries fringing the Mediterranean suggest a light bag of man-made fibres which can be washed readily. Summer and extended season camping in the British Isles or northern Europe will call for a cheaper down bag of zero degree Centigrade comfort.

However, the enemy weight comes looming around the corner again whenever we discuss sleeping bags. Top quality down gives the best weight and bulk for warmth value, but costs are high.

Man-made fibres are relatively cheap; they are also bulky and used to be poor insulators. But great strides have been made by the chemists and engineers since the first edition of this book appeared and firstly I will discuss these materials before going on to Nature's own methods.

War, while horrible to contemplate in the particular, does give an enormous incentive to better-off nations to develop materials which will enable their troops to fight in atrocious conditions and be in a better position to vanquish the enemy. So it was with man-made fibre insulations. After the Korean war, the United States realized that very often the army that had warm troops had the upper edge, for cold, lack of proper food and incessant rain soon demoralizes all but the dedicated fighter. Accordingly it stock-piled thousands of tons of top quality down against a future war.

When its armies began fighting in Vietnam, under conditions entirely different from Korea, reports soon filtered back from Intelligence that down clothing and sleeping-bags were almost useless in a country that was wet as well as cold in the mountains. Cut to chemical laboratories. Scene one: scientists re-examine their inventory of fibres—some of which had never been put into production. Hurried tests. No improvement.

Scene two: engineers, grappling with a knitting machine that had gone haywire and had crimped up the yarn, sit cursing. Bright engineer grabs handful of bulked up crimped yarn, shouts cowboy oath. Explains to tired colleagues his discovery.

The scenario is apocryphal, but I know the idea for modern man-made insulation fibres for clothing did come from the panti-hose and tights research and development laboratories.

When tights are knitted the yarn is given its elasticity by two tiny wheels running at different speeds as the fibre passes over. This sets a permanent crimp in the thread and when knitted it shrivels the garment to about a third of its size. This same idea was used with other fibres and it was found that a fibre with a deep crimp could bulk up in a great frothy cloud, yet be capable of being compressed. The crimp is heat-set into the fibre and so it wants to return to its bulked state once the pressure is released.

At first there was no proper method of retaining the bulk of fibre in one place—down bunches too, but soon separates when shaken. So the fibre was given a fine coating of plastic to make a batt. This merely added to the weight and bulk. Now the best fibres are quilted to a backing and this works quite well. Two layers of the stuff, with the quilting stitches separated, produces the cloth.

Why man-made fibres for Vietnam—and now backpacking? Well, being a plastic fibre mechanically crimped, it will not absorb water and collapse as will down. You can wear a properly crimped fibre garment or lie in a sleeping-bag and become almost soaked before the main insulative qualities—the retention of large air voids—are lost. One up for the scientists—especially after the price of good quality down went soaring when the United States began stock-piling.

Are the products—sleeping bags and shell clothing—as good as down-filled items? Here we come to much subjectivity in the arguments. On the minus side: properly crimped man-made fibres do not compress as much as down of equal weight. This results in a bulkier package or a heavier package. On the plus side: no more sodden down sleeping bags that never dry out and lose their in-sulation properties. No more loss of fine down through a small tear. No more sneezing for those with allergies. Lower costs, longer life. No storage problems—they don't suffer from damp or lack of airing. Chris Bonnington and the boys have used them in the Himalayas and discovered they stood up to hard usage and yet still retained their insulation.

For myself, I am almost converted—I grew up in the era of down filling and I find it rather difficult to break the habit, but I can attest to having used man-made fibres shamelessly for some years now and I have been very pleased on several occasions. I once fell in a river and soaked my kit just before dark. I wrung out the bag and swirled it around my head, got in with some dread and after a while I was warm and I remained so overnight awaking to a dry bag in the morning. Down could never have done that.

But as with all things, you have to buy well. Short of cutting open a bag there is no way of really telling how it is made inside, so the only criterion I can pass on regarding man-made fibre bags is to look to the label. If it says do not dry clean it is probable the filling is bonded in a batt by a binder which will dissolve in the cleaning flued. Reject it. The best guide is to seek a reputable sleeping-bag-maker's list and see what he proposes. His reputation rests on his product and he will not destroy a business for the sake of being fashionable, or just plain old cheap.

Choosing a sleeping bag demands much care because there are many inferior bags around. A sleeping bag, together with your packframe and tent are the biggest expenditures which must be made for full enjoyment of your hobby, so do not rush into buying the first bag you see.

Having first decided the type of bag you need—cold weather, temperate or subtropical—go and see some examples at the nearest high quality outfitter's shop. Make sure the down used in the good quality bag of your choice is new and contains no second-hand reclaimed down, contains no feather for 'bulking' and has been properly stored where it cannot pick up unpleasant smells.

I once tested a reputable bag and woke nauseated the first night out. The horrible smell of scorched feather was so bad I had to get up and get dressed. So ask to see a down bag of your fancy, pat it hard several times and look closely around the stitching to see if any quill is showing through. Then bury your nose deep inside and see if it smells sweetly. Look closely *all* over for the quality of the cutting and stitching—suspect it if you see loose threads. Make sure that any down bag is not through-sewn but is made with either box, slant box or overlapping tube construction to eliminate cold spots. A through-sewn bag is sure to be cold where the insulation is pinched by the stitching.

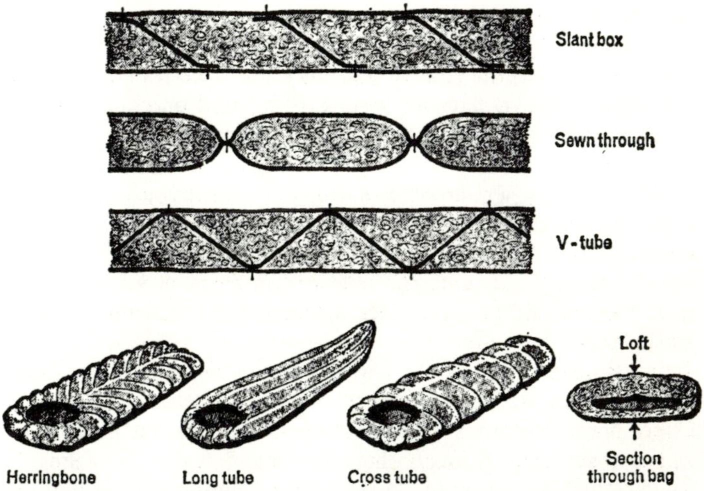

Figure 3. *Some of the terms used in sleeping bag manufacture*

Free loft is usually considered to be an indication of the quality of a bag—remember thickness is warmth. But some manufacturers achieve free loft by introducing a little curled feather with the down filling to give bulk in a new bag. After a while the 'stalk' crushes and the free loft is reduced. Quills of the feather poke through the covering and are lost. Reject any fill other than down for a bag to give a long service life.

After satisfying yourself on all these points, stuff the down bag into its sack, and using your own pocket scales, weigh it. Anything less than 2 pounds 3 ounces is of little value except in high summer. More than 3 pounds 8 ounces is too much for temperate use. Heavier bags which look bulky when unfolded could be filled with a mixture containing feathers.

The next job is to measure the length and *internal* girth of the bag.

For a person of average height a sleeping bag should not be less than 78 inches long—90 inches if you are a six-footer. The girth for average height should be at least 48 inches where your pelvis will lie. When the weather turns cold you should be able to snuggle right down inside your bag comfortably and leave only your nose and mouth exposed. A short bag will prevent this. *Buy the bag you have examined and not a similar one from stock.*

A box-shaped toe-end to the bag gives maximum insulation around the feet. A flat end besides being cold on cold nights will prevent you wiggling your toes to relax your feet after a long day in walking boots.

Sleeping bags get dirty no matter how much you try to protect them. Any food spilled onto a sleeping bag must be wiped away immediately. Even the smallest snag or tear will allow precious down to ooze through so cover the hole with a patch of sticking plaster from the first aid kit or a piece of vinyl tape until you can do the job properly.

To keep the inside of the bag as clean as possible for as long as possible there are cotton and nylon removable liners on sale. But I have never had any success with these contraptions because they will not stay put through the night and I wake up feeling like Houdini making an escape bid. My own solution may sound kinky but it is efficient and you can try it for yourself according to your inclination.

I pack two pairs of women's tights—the type which has an extra gusset in the seat section. They weigh little but when worn in the sleeping bag give complete freedom to move legs around in bed while allowing no skin contact with the nylon shell of the bag. I also wear a cotton T-shirt in bed which keeps my trunk from soiling the inside of the bag too. The tights are easily washed as are the T-shirts.

Tights seem to have the ability to help regulate the heat flow of the body—warm on cold nights and yet not too hot when it is warm. In company with many mountain boys, water skiers, pot-holers and dinghy sailors, I wear women's tights as insulation. They are good under trousers when the wind is particularly keen.

A sleeping bag is only efficient when it is quite dry. Yet paradoxically it must 'breathe' to allow quite a sizeable volume of moisture to evaporate from the body. A lot of this moisture is still locked up in the bag when you rise in the morning, therefore if you are to have another comfortable night that evening you must ensure the bag is thoroughly aired before it is stuffed away for the day.

When the sun is shining or there is a wind blowing, airing is no problem. Ten minutes inside and out in the sunshine will clear up the moisture still locked in the down. When the weather is bad one has to do the best one can. Turn the bag inside out on rising and get as much air all round it under the cover of the tent and stuff it into its sack as the last job before striking camp. Failure to do this simple chore will ensure a cold night the next time the bag is used.

Long term storage of a good sleeping bag with down filling should not be under compression. Shake the bag out and hang it up in a wardrobe for the winter and this will extend the life of the miraculous down filaments. And always shake out the bag on making camp to allow the down to fully expand before use.

When the bag has become soiled, take it to a reputable dry cleaning company and have the best cleaning job they can offer. When it is returned hang it up in the sunshine out of doors, for a couple of days at least, to rid it of all the cleaning fluid fumes. People have died in newly cleaned sleeping bags which have not been properly aired.

Before leaving sleeping bags, let me warn you against the temptation of buying a bag which has a ground sheet sewn to it. These are the invention of the devil because they cannot be properly aired. Forget about them. There is no such thing as a waterproof sleeping bag.

SLEEPING PADS

Wherever your body weight compresses the filling on any sleeping bag, be it down or man-made fibre, practically all insulation is lost and the ground will conduct your body heat away without restriction. Therefore you must be properly insulated underneath. Perhaps you have heard the adage, "Two thirds of the bedding underneath you and one third on top for a comfortable night". This ancient camper's rite was another way of saying you need insulation underneath your body when sleeping.

The lightest and cheapest insulation is newspaper. Take a walk by the Temple underground station in London any winter's night and you will see the dead-beats of the City gathered in their regular sleeping place. Underneath each one is newspaper collected during the afternoon and early evening from the litter boxes which line the Strand and Fleet Street. Tramps have long known of the value of newspaper as insulation.

If you are travelling light through settled areas where people live you can either buy your own newspaper or gather it as you go tramp style. Try and get as much thickness as possible under your body area, legs lose less heat.

If this sounds too much of a fag or you are travelling where there are not likely to be any newsvendors, you will need to carry some insulation with you. Fortunately, plastic foam of various sorts is not overly heavy.

All the best manufacturers both sell a special kind of sleeping pad which is made from a closed cell plastic foam. This type of cell is not open-joined to the next so it takes up no moisture—except a slight amount on the surface where the tiny cells are improperly formed.

These special pads are only about half an inch thick but have a tremendous insulative value. They can be used at meal stops to sit on and laid under the tent floor in the position where the sleeping bag will be laid out at night. Although they do give some comfort it is still advisable to form a small depression where the hip bone will lie.

Closed cell sleeping pads are the lightest proper insulation you can buy. Unfortunately they are awkward. But if you have a large stuff bag for your pack frame, the pad will roll up inside the stuff bag and still leave room for slipping the sleeping bag in its own stuff sack inside. The Karrimor pad is made to fold in the middle to slip down the inside of a rucksack.

Sleeping pads of this sort are comparatively cheap and weigh about 9 ounces. And unless you have some other form of insulation they are indispensable.

Luxury lightweighting comes with the use of a short airbed. There are several around. Some are traditionally built with two sheets of ruberized canvas welded into reeds and pillow. There is, however, a much better idea which has individual reeds which stuff inside pockets formed between two pieces of nylon material. There is also a full-length nylon material box section mattress. Take your pick—remember you have to carry it.

The choice of insulation is dictated not only by your pocket but more especially by the all-up weight you are willing to carry. To begin with I suggest you invest in a closed cell sleeping pad.

Having now discussed the basics: packframe or rucksack, shelter, sleeping bag, wet weather clothing and insulation, we can turn to other components of your kit.

FIRST AID BOX

There is no such thing as a perfect first aid kit. So much depends on what you are planning to do with your travelling, whether you are accident prone, and where you are going.

The least you are likely to run into are blisters, a small burn, a small cut or abrasion, upset stomach, grit in the eye, and perhaps a sprain. The worst we hope will never happen, but I will discuss first aid and accidents in a later chapter.

To cover the minor emergencies it is essential that you keep salves and physics in a handy place in a container which can easily be opened single handed. Always keep your kit in the same outside pocket of your rucksack or packframe so that it can be reached for instinctively.

If you are travelling in temperate zones where people are not far away, obviously you can make do with a sachet of sticking plasters stuffed in a shirt pocket. In wilderness country this must be increased to simple remedies to cover other emergencies such as burns, stings and gastric disorders. Far off the trail medicines will be needed by those who intend to cover large distances—especially in foreign countries where medicine is more like witch doctoring—and expensive.

In every first aid kit there should be a small mirror. This handy tool not only allows you to see if your hair is tidy and beard trimmed, but it can be used to examine an eye which is contaminated by grit or an insect; examine a sore throat. In a real emergency it can be used as a signalling device if the sun is up—the sun's reflection from a two-inch square mirror can be seen half a dozen miles away.

As a general duty kit I would suggest you start with some or all of the following:

1 25g tube of 'Savlon' (ICI) for burns, cuts, abrasions, etc.
100 ml bottle of 'Optone' for soothing sun or snow tired eyes, irritants, etc.
1 small 'Paragon' plain wound dressing
1 sachet of 'Band-aid' washproof dressing strip

1 small pack of gauze dressing
1 small roll 'Micropore' surgical adhesive tape
1 small plastic tablet tube containing 10 aspirin or Paracetamol tablets, labelled
1 small pack of 'Purazone' water treatment tablets
1 small mirror, glass or metal
1 pair of nail clippers
1 half-used 25g tube of 'Anthisan' (M & B) for insect or jellyfish stings and bites
1 small tube of insect repellent—I prefer Cutters

This simple list will cover most minor problems and it should all be packed snugly into a polythene box with a snap-on lid. Make sure the lid can be removed single-handed. An elastic band around the box will keep the contents secure.

In the kit can go a piece of card into which have been buried three sewing needles. Around this card wind several three yard lengths of thread and also attach a couple of medium-sized safety pins.

The kit is also a good place to keep a spare torch bulb and a polythene bag containing a supply of good foot powder such as 'Mycil—A'.

For those going foreign—especially to hot climates and Mediterranean countries—the kit should be increased to contain a short course of wide-band antibiotics (your doctor can prescribe them for you) and a five-day course of 'Streptotriad' tablets to cure incessant diarrhoea. Salt tablets are needed for travel in very hot climates.

A small plastic bottle of 'Lomotil' will also bring relief from diarrhoea and excessive bowel activity through poor water supply or indifferent food. Medical opinion suggests that pre-courses of tablets for traveller's diarrhoea are of unproven value and can, in fact, produce the symptoms of the very thing they are supposed to prevent!

If there are sea voyages involved and you are a traveller who needs sedatives, do not forget to take enough for the return voyage. For high altitude and snow-line travel add glacier crêmes to the kit.

The idea of a first aid kit is to be as small as practicable and as varied as possible. The above kit should not cost more than £1 including the box and will weigh about 6 ounces. Always replace any items used after a trip so that there is always a full supply of a vital material if needed.

WHISTLE

A whistle attached to a lanyard of fine nylon cord should always be worn around the neck when travelling off the beaten track. The most penetrating whistle is a nickel-silver pea type sold under the brand of 'Butterfly'. THE INTERNATIONAL SIGNAL OF DISTRESS IN THE MOUNTAINS IS SIX BLASTS BLOWN AT INTERVALS OF ONE MINUTE.

KNIFE

A knife attracts much discussion because it is such a personal and subjective object of utility. Some swear by sheath knives, others by the faithful clasp. Others go for the 'Original Swiss Army Knife' because it has so many gadgets and others simply take one from the kitchen drawer. I will leave the selection to your fancy but ask you to consider these few points before buying.

Will it be safe when not in use? Can it be honed to a keen edge and kept that way? Is it heavy enough to fashion tent pegs, poles, fireside implements? If it folds will the blade lock in the open position?

I personally like a folding clasp knife with a slightly rockered blade which allows for cutting up meat on a flat piece of wood. The blade is of carbon steel and keeps a good edge although it will rust if not regularly attended to. The handle has a hooked end for a positive grip even in cold weather. The blade is about 3½ inches long and it is firm enough to split wood and do quite heavy cutting. It has a staple on one end to which is attached a lanyard of nylon cord so that I am not likely to lose it.

I also carry a small slip stone in a tiny polythene bag. The stone was soaked in oil before I used it and I can keen up the knife blade regularly. Remember that it is usually blunt knives that cut fingers!

COMPASS

If you are likely to be travelling away from settled country; over moorland tracks or high ground prone to be shrouded in mist at any time—and this includes the Pennine Way and Offa's Dyke—you will need to carry a compass with you at all times. Take a look at the Silva range of pocket compasses and you will surely find one to suit your taste. The point to remember is how simple will it be in use? Practise regularly so that you can use a compass in adverse conditions should you ever need to (see chapter 4).

EMERGENCY MATCH SUPPLY

Buy a couple of boxes of Bryant and May's Windproof Flamers and search the household medical cabinet for any empty 'Anadin' can with a plastic snap-on lid or find an empty 35 mm film can with plastic lid. Decant the matches and tear off both sides of the striker and stow the whole lot in the can. Now hide this supply down at the bottom of your rucksack or packsack.

Always replace matches which have been used after each trip.

PORTABLE FIRE

It would be nice to rely on an open fire wherever we went. At least that is the way I feel. But I must admit that open fires are not always practicable and the more travellers who get around the open paths and countryside the more the pressure there is going to be on natural fuels.

Therefore it is necessary to consider the choice of some form of portable fire which is suitable for the lightweighter.

This choice breaks down into three groups, solid fuel, liquid fuel and liquid petroleum gas (LPG).

In the first group there are a number of proprietary makes of solid fuel tablets and jellified methylated spirits. To my mind they can all be dismissed for serious cooking simply because none can give the amount of heat necessary to cook efficiently in the open air. As starters for pressure paraffin stoves, solid fuel tablets have their place. As fire starters when wood is damp, there is nothing surer than a solid fuel tablet. But for cooking a stew or a dish of bacon and eggs they are next to useless.

The famous 'Tommy's Cooker'—a tin of jellified methylated spirits with a crude tinplate windshield—might just find pack-room as an emergency stove, but that is all. Weight for weight, none of these devices comes close to a pressure stove or a LPG stove for heat output.

When we discuss liquid-fuelled stoves the range widens immediately.

Firstly there is the little Swiss-made brass alcohol stove which burns methlyated spirits. But I will dismiss this for the same reasons as the previous section.

I have long carried a SeAb 'Stormcooker' which comprises two cooking pots, a lid-cum-frypan, a special two-piece windshield and an alcohol stove. It worked very well, although rather thirsty for meths. It weighs 2 pounds 2 ounces, but this includes the weight of a canteen. It is the only alcohol stove I know which can be used for serious cooking. Then comes the pressure stoves burning either petrol or paraffin. The simplest and lightest stove on the market in this category is the Borde bomb. It weighs 8 ounces, has a brass tube with a filler at one end and vaporizer/burner at the other. It loads with petrol and is self-pressurizing.

The Borde bomb is either loved or hated. Many mountain men swear by it—others, including myself, would not give it pack room. I mention it because it is the lightest true pressure stove I know of.

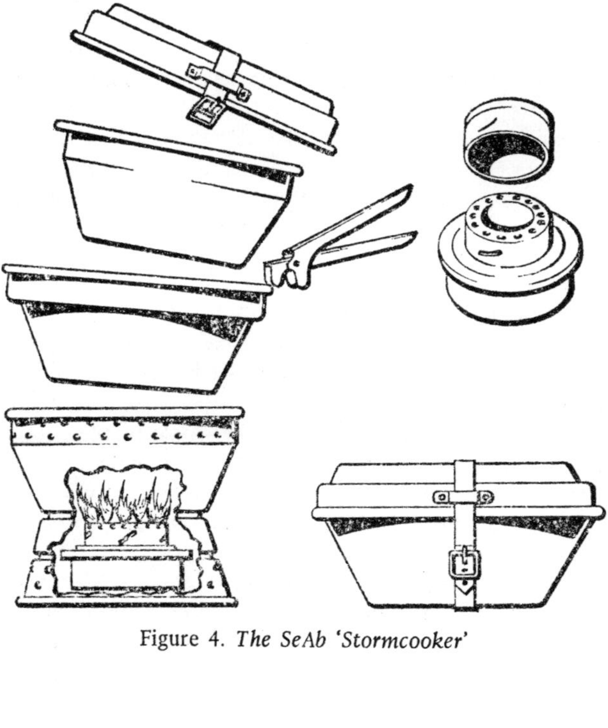

Figure 4. *The SeAb 'Stormcooker'*

Next there are two tried and tested stoves which are very popular with lightweighters—the SVEA 123 and the Primus 71L, both of which are petrol-fuelled.

The SVEA comes with a brass windshield and tiny aluminium cooking pot. It loads with ⅓ pint of petrol and weighs 1 pound 2 ounces.

The Primus 71L is slightly larger and comes in a tinplate carrying case which also forms a windshield. It weighs 1 pound 6 ounces and charges with ½ pint of fuel.

Moving up the scale there is the Primus 8R and the bigger Optimus 111B. Both of these designs are similar; a folding steel box with petrol tank and burner inside. A trivet folds into place as the windshield lid is raised. The Primus 8R weighs 1 pound 9 ounces and produces a very efficient flame. It burns leaded or unleaded petrol. The Optimus 111B weighs 3 pounds 9 ounces and there is a paraffin-burning model of the same size.

Do make sure the heat shield is in the proper place before use—other wise the heat shield will become a heat conductor with pyrotechnical results—and it is a good habit to remove the control knob once the flame has been trimmed. This saves it from being trodden on.

Still on the market and as popular as ever is the original classic Pocket Primus model 96/6. It runs on paraffin and weighs 1 pound 12 ounces empty and with a half pint charge will burn approximately 2 hours. It will boil a quart of water in seven minutes at sea level in sheltered conditions.

All of these stoves I have used extensively and the fact that they have stood the test of many years of use by hundreds of thousands of travellers shows how reliable and popular they are.

There is only one major drawback to each of them—the need to keep volatile or smelly reserves of fuel in the pack. One small spillage of fuel is enough to contaminate the whole of the contents of the pack and a paraffin taint is almost impossible to eradicate. Petrol stoves are self-pre-heating but paraffin stoves need an extra pre-heating fuel of either solid fuel tablets or methylated spirits.

On balance I would choose the SVEA 123 for solo lightweighting and Optimus 8R for twosomes. The fuel I would carry in an aluminium Markill flask of ¾ litre capacity or any perfectly sealing metal flask. To prevent contamination of the pack, I always carry the stove and flask in a separate sack lashed to the outside of the main pack.

The big advantage to all these stoves is the availability of the fuel supply—almost universal for petrol and paraffin, or kerosene nearly so. Spares are obtainable throughout most of Europe, and North America.

Turning to LPG stoves there is an ever-widening choice. The Camping Gaz Bleuet S200 is so universal that no introduction is necessary. It weighs 1 pound 12 ounces and its cartridges can be obtained just about everywhere in the civilized world.

The S200 has one major disadvantage. The cartridge is pierced by the regulator valve when first inserted and cannot be removed without danger until the cartridge is exhausted. Since the fuel is butane, which boils at minus 1°C, there is tendency for the stove to cease to function efficiently when the temperature dips towards freezing. A fresh cartridge would pep things up but the half-used cartridge cannot be removed. Wrapping warm hands around the cartridge helps vaporizing a little but chills the fingers.

There are LPG stoves with removable self-sealing screw-in cartridges. Tilley Go-gas and Primus make these more sophisticated models. Primus has a wide distribution in Scandinavia and Tilley is well known in Britain but not so much abroad.

There are two other British makes with self-sealing non-screw-in cartridges, Veritas and Parasene. The valve is opened by patent needle but the cartridge clips into place.

So far as cooking speeds and efficiency are concerned there is little to choose between any of the LPG stoves on the market. One handy small stove which used to be made by Primus—the Grasshopper—has now gone out of production, although manufacturer's stocks are still being cleared by another company.

I personally rejected the S200 for the reasons I have given and I bought a Tilley Go-gas stove. It weighed slightly less than the S200 and quite a lot less than the Primus 2221, but it had one big advantage, it could be used on its own Go-gas cartridges of 6-ounce capacity as well as Primus 2201 9-ounce and 2202 16-ounce cartridges.

The Tilley stove has a combined windshield and trivet and when fitted to its own or a Primus 2202 cartridge it is very stable.

To my mind, the ideal LPG stove for lightweighters has yet to be designed. The Bleuet comes close for stability and availability, and the Tilley Go-gas for flexibility, but none are so economical as petrol or paraffin stoves.

The big advantages of any LPG stove are instant lighting, closer control of the flame, and no risk of contamination from fuel spillage.

These have to be offset against the high cost of LPG fuel, poor burning at low temperatures, and availability of fuel cartridges when compared with petrol and paraffin.

My choice of LPG stove would be governed by the journey to be undertaken. The Continent is dominated by Camping Gaz, so I would choose the S200 because there would normally be no freeze-up problems. In Britain or Scandinavia I would choose the Tilley Go-gas stove and use the more economical Primus 2202 cartridge.

My choice between liquid fuel stoves and LPG is not easy, but on balance I would come down in favour of LPG for summer use simply because of its handiness. For winter travel, and travel to cold zones in summer, I would opt for petrol burning liquid fuelled stoves. Do make sure you know the local name for petrol or paraffin in any foreign country through which you are likely to be travelling. Ignorance is at least likely to bring frustration—at worst an explosion.

Like tents, there is no such thing as the ideal stove, and reference should be made to the test table in Appendix III. Incidentally, all the LPG stove makers produce gas mantled lanterns to run off their cartridges; worth considering for winter camping.

POTS AND PANS

The choice of a canteen—as we call cooking pots in Britain—is wide. But bearing in mind the enemy weight is lurking around again, I shall limit my discussion to two well-proven units—one for solo travel and one for twosomes.

These two canteens are made of aluminium by 'Bulldog' and are called 'Hobo' for the solo unit and 'Rover' for the twosome. Each is well made in spun metal and contains a saucepan with lid, a frying pan and shallow pan which can be used as a plate.

The Hobo unit has a fry pan with a steel handle which snaps over to lock the nest together. I drilled my handle with lightening holes and saved some weight, but the set as bought weighs 1 pound without mug. The saucepan is one pint capacity and doubles as a kettle having a steel wire bail which snaps into the upright position to make pouring reasonably easy. An empty saucepan can be used to carry fresh eggs well wrapped in newspaper.

The Rover canteen is similar to the Hobo but bigger. There is no folding handle to the fry pan—a separate pot gripper is provided which is quite satisfactory except that it marks the rim of the plate and fry pan after extended use. The saucepan is 2½-pint capacity with a similar steel wire bail. The Rover outfit weighs 1 pound 4 ounces and has no spare metal to remove to save weight.

If you own both canteens, I recommend you take the Hobo saucepan nested inside the Rover canteen when going as a twosome. This gives more flexibility in cooking arrangements. The Hobo saucepan or billy is available as a separate item.

There is an even lighter outfit than the Hobo, called the Hiker canteen. But I found the gauge of the aluminium was so thin that I was forever burning food before it was properly cooked, so I do not recommend it.

One old favourite which has been with the Scout movement for years is the Cookwell canteen. It falls nicely between the Hobo and Rover as a bigger-than-one-not-quite-two outfit and weighs 1 pound.

It is a good idea to get a PU-proofed nylon bag with drawstring just big enough to take your canteen. This 'dirty pot' bag will save open fire soot from soiling your kit. Remember it is a mistake to scour pots inside and out to produce polished aluminium each wash-up. The black patina on the outside of used pots transfers heat quicker than a polished surface and thus saves fuel.

CUTLERY

You already have a knife, no need to take a table knife on your lightweight travels. Similarly, forks are a refinement of the settled house dweller. All that is needed is a dessert spoon. The trick is to cut all food to bite size—Chinese cook-style—before cooking, and the spoon will transfer everything to your hungry mouth with ease. There are some very good cheap stainless steel dessert spoons around these days—buy the lightest one you can find.

I have used an implement called the 'Eazie Eater'. It is a cross between a spoon, a fork and a knife. As you would guess, it does none of the jobs efficiently and does not fall happily to the mouth either unless you polish off the sharp corners with 'wet-and-dry' paper. You will also need a 'Baby' can opener and perhaps an 'Oasis' combined corkscrew, crown cork and beer can opener.

WATER CARRIER

You will find it necessary to carry water with you from time to time. The most satisfactory way I have discovered is to carry it in a one-gallon-sized collapsible bottle made from polythene. When empty it takes up hardly any space at all. When full it holds a gallon without risk of spillage. Although it fills easily enough at a tap it is not so easy to fill from a mountain stream.

MUGS

Choose a one pint polythene mug if you do not mind drinking out of plastics. It keeps hot drinks hot for longer periods than aluminium when used in exposed places, does not burn the lips, weighs only 2½ ounces and can be scratched with marks at ⅓, ½ and ⅔ pint to help when re-constituting dehydrated foods. Do not choose less than one pint even if you feel this quantity is too much for you. A long drink from one stove burn is more economical than a second brew-up with smaller quantities. A big mug is also useful for soups on cold days.

Tea making is done right in the mug with tea bags doused in boiling water.

FOOD BOXES

Polythene food boxes sold in Woolworths and other multiple stores are fine for lightweighting providing the lids snap on securely. Remember that round lids are always a better fit than rectangular or square shapes. I would suggest that one sandwich sized box will hold all your perishable foods and a similar sized box will store your bread substitutes.

Look for the famous Green Top screw cap polyjars in any good camping shop and buy one small and one ½-litre size. The latter makes a good storage jar and can be used to reconstitute dehydrated foods while walking. The smaller is fine for holding cooking oil without leaking.

Most of your storage will be done in polythene bags with wire twist closures. Make sure you have plenty on hand before leaving for a trip.

ODDS AND ENDS

Washing up and washing out socks and underclothes is a necessary chore which cannot be ignored. It can be done in a square of vinyl sheeting about 24 inches along one side. In soft soil you can scrape a shallow depression and lay the vinyl into it, anchoring the corners with large stones. This forms a bowl in which the necessary washing can be done. The method adds only a couple of ounces to your load and is adequate for overnight hiking.

Longer trips demand a little more civilizing and I suggest a small plastic washing-up bowl about 14 inches across—Woolworths and most good hardware stores sell them. They are flexible and pack well and weigh about 4 ounces. But the increased comfort a bowl brings is out of all proportion to its weight.

Another way is to buy a cheap plastic bucket—the type with a rounded bottom—and using your sharp knife score round the bucket about 3 inches up. It is a simple job to clamp your knife onto a brick on a table and pressing the bucket against the blade keep rotating until a complete circle is formed. Saw along this line.

Most big supermarkets sell a tiny pan scourer and sponge made by '3M' which is very light and does a good job of cleaning up even the worst burned pot. The sponge part makes the most of miniscule quantities of detergent. And as for detergent, I carry a tube of Dylon which not only deals with washing dishes but is good for rinsing out underclothes, socks and handkerchiefs. It works quite well even in salt water scooped from the sea. As the tube is used up I squeeze from the bottom and cut off the redundant section sealing the end by turning it over. This saves excess weight.

Cordage is something no self-respecting backpacker should be without. I suggest you buy three or four lengths of nylon cord of light gauge. Each length should be about 15 feet. Heat seal the ends to prevent fraying and neatly hank them up so they don't get into a bird's nest. This gauge of cord comes in for all sorts of uses from making new bootlaces to storm guys, from linen lines to rigging bivvies, as well as the odd lashing job on the packframe.

TORCH

Artificial lighting is always a problem for the lightweighter. Batteries are heavy and they seem to become exhausted more quickly than when weight is no problem. In summer, in 50° latitudes, there is little need of powerful lighting at night. A small flashlight will cover most eventualities, such as finding items in the tent, viewing sign-posts, reading maps and so on. In high summer in northern latitudes there is hardly a need for a torch at all—even in Scotland. In Spain, Portugal, Italy, North Africa and the Middle East, darkness comes early and stays around late in the morning, so a bigger torch is desirable—especially if you intend to travel in the cool of the night.

Winter camping brings fresh problems about lighting. Darkness can be around for 12 hours or more and even cooking has to be done at night. Cold weather saps the power of electric batteries and renewal of the cells is more frequent than in summer.

I have torches and lamps for all types of camping. For weekend and summer hiking I use the Ever Ready Minilight. It runs on two HP7 cells and I carry a spare set, with a spare bulb in the first aid kit. At a pinch I can rob a pair out of my small transistor radio.

I drilled a small hole in the side of the plastic casing of the torch and made a fine nylon cord lanyard to prevent it being dropped and lost in long growth in the dark. Used intelligently, this little torch, which weighs just over two ounces, is quite adequate for emergency pathfinding and general duties in camp. By intelligent use, I mean that it is only switched on in short bursts when absolutely necessary. Continuous use would exhaust it in about ten minutes—a few seconds at a time gives the batteries a chance to recover and several nights of duty.

There is another kind of battery on the market which takes up the same space as an HP7 cell which will last hours. Called the Mallory AA Duracell—Ever Ready sells them too (MN 1500)—this manganese alkaline battery costs over three times as much as an HP7 but gives a very long life and better recovery. During daylight, reverse one of the batteries so they are both bottom up. This prevents accidental switch-on draining your precious batteries.

For winter use I accept the bigger burden and use a two cell unit modelled on the old US Army torch, called a Scout torch. It has a lamp unit at right angles to the body, gives a powerful pre-focused beam and can be obtained with different lenses. There is a clip to hook it onto a belt. It weighs 11 ounces and uses two SP2 cells, or Duracells.

I also have a tiny Chinese hurricane lamp which weighs only 12 ounces and burns paraffin. This little old-fashioned gem adds warmth and light to a tent on a dark stormy winter's night and burns for over ten hours on one quarter pint filling. The trick when moving each day is to charge the lamp with only about two tablespoonsful of fuel and empty away what remains each morning. There is, however, a fire risk, which must be continuously borne in mind in the cramped living space when two people share a small lightweight tent. The same goes for candles.

If you choose candles as a standby, buy what used to be called 'carriage candles'. They are a harder wax—stearin—and last longer. Being stubby they are less likely to be upset. Always 'spot' the bottom with a match and set them in the saucepan of your canteen if you take them inside a tent. Any falling wax and heat will be caught by the aluminium can. Keep well away from nylon walls. Candles give a surprising amount of warmth and quickly snug up a small tent in the first chills of autumn.

MAPS

To my mind, maps are not only objects of utility but sources of great pleasure. I read maps like other people read novels, poring over them in the long winter months and idle hours imprisoned on trains and airliners. A map is more than just an indication of a road or pathway but framework on which the outdoors life is spun.

We in Britain have the finest maps in the world, published by the Ordnance Survey Office at Southampton. There are OS maps in all manner of scales and for all manner of purposes. All other British maps published privately are based on the surveys of the Ordnance Survey which should be confirmation enough of the value of our inheritance from the old military map-makers such as General Roy.

For all practical purposes the walker in Britain can buy no better maps than those produced by the Ordnance Survey and sold by its accredited agents. There is one of these metricated treasure houses to cover all parts of the country and they are continually being updated. As well as the standard series there are a number of sheets covering the National Parks in England and Scotland and there is a special sheet covering Snowdonia.

Hitch-hikers should find the double-sided Ordnance Survey route-planner maps of great value for travel in England, Wales and Scotland. With the covers removed for weight saving these excellent maps are the best indication of through, trunk and classified link roads and show most towns above 600 inhabitants.

For close exploration of a local area there are maps on 2½-inch and 6-inch scales.

For travel in Ireland—including Ulster—buy quarter-inch scale maps from the Irish Ordnance Survey Office in Dublin or any good map seller.

Travel in France means Michelin maps—and very good they are too. For most other countries in Europe I use the maps published by Shell. Despite their rather large size they do give a wealth of information, although they lack topography and the high standard of detail found on British Ordnance Survey sheets.

The point about map buying is to make sure that you have the right one for the area you intend to travel. Always look at the bottom right-hand corner of the sheet and you will find the imprint and the date of publication. Buy the latest you can secure—maps go out of date from the day they are published and in these modern days of high technology you might find a motorway or dockland right on the idyllic spot you have chosen in advance for a quiet weekend away.

Incidentally, one way to gather a good map library is to ask all the family to buy one of your choice at birthdays and high days: the cost is only a small sum but if non-map readers could only understand the thought behind it they would buy you more!

There are further ideas about map reading and finding your way in chapter 4.

CLOTHING

With most of the kit out of the way I will turn to the most unexciting but the most important section of equipment.

Right from the start we have to know what we are about when we dress—fashions apart it is simple to maintain the body at its optimum temperature—98·4° on the Fahrenheit scale. For air temperatures above this we have to dress in such a way that excess heat can be conducted away to the atmosphere as quickly as possible. Below this 'normal' temperature we have to don clothes to prevent too much heat loss.

There is no better primary way of maintaining body heat than a proper diet of enough calories for the system to burn off. Moderate loads of say 25 pounds carried in temperate climates suggest a 3,500 calories a day intake. But more about this in the chapter on cookery. Let's assume you have a proper diet, what then? The pores open and close to allow the continual escape of excess heat produced by the body at work in the form of moisture vapour which must find its way to the atmosphere. Otherwise sweating, overheating and distress sets in—try moving around in a skin-tight rubber suit for a while to test this theory.

Clothing has to perform two functions, insulation and controlled conduction of excess heat, in the form of moisture vapour, away from the skin surface. Moreover, variations in activity change the rates of the two functions so the clothing has to be very flexible—not just bendy but capable of infinite adaptation to suit the functions.

Most experienced backpackers have now settled for the layer method of dressing. Next to the skin they have a layer which will vent away body moisture. Because there are various zones on the body radiating different temperatures—the head, crotch and the axilla or under-arms are hottest, with extremities the coolest—there is no universal garment to match all conditions.

So the first layer is usually underpants and T-shirt or vest of open-weave cotton—most polyester fabrics do not vent very well and should be considered second best to cotton.

Above this layer should come a denser cellular layer through which moisture can escape but in which heat is retained. Wool is best, light woollen trousers and a light lambswool sweater are just fine. Again polyester fabrics are generally second best.

If the body still feels cold, another thicker layer of wool or cellular knitted polyester fabric is needed. Venting is again very necessary. Thickness alone guarantees insulation—the thicker the layer the warmer you will be.

Finally comes the water-proof layer which I have already discussed under the section on the cagoule and over-trousers.

After trial and error I have finally settled for a rig composed of an openweave T-shirt and comfortable underpants—taking care to eliminate any tightness or looseness which might cause chafing. Over this goes a light, long sleeved lambswool sweater and wool/polyester trousers cut fairly full in the seat and not 'fashionable' in the town sense. Finally comes a heavy Scottish woollen mackinaw shirt with two breast pockets and of coat length. This is worn outside the trouser band.

As the day warms up I unbutton and eventually doff the mackinaw and strip right down to the T-shirt in really hot weather. I never feel distressed because by buttoning or unbuttoning the mackinaw I can control the ventilation. Moisture-laden air from around my body flows up through the open neck welt of the sweater or mackinaw collar and ventilating air is drawn in through the open bottom of the mackinaw.

To my mind, anoraks as sold by camp clothiers are the invention of the devil and have only one advantage—extra pockets. A heavy windproof cloth prevents proper venting and proper transfer of body moisture, and it lacks the necessary thickness. The drawstring around the waist prevents ventilating air from rising over the whole of the trunk and the front cannot be fully opened to give a final stage ventilation before removing—as with a following wind. The original Eskimo anorak was a much better piece of equipment and it is a pity clothiers do not go back and have another look at the garment they have maligned so much to see where they went wrong.

For colder weather I wear a loose-fitting down-filled waistcoat over the whole rig to give another 2½ inches of thickness. I do not go high up so I have no need for expensive and excessive duvet clothing. I bought a Point Five waistcoat with a small collar which I also wear in my sleeping bag on very cold nights. I have already mentioned the use of women's tights as insulators under woollen trousers and these cellular lightweight garments are excellent for venting the leg pores without their losing much valuable heat when the air temperature is low.

I reject jeans as a walker's trouser. They are tough and unyielding, made of densely woven cotton so lack air cells, and flap miserably when wet below the knees. Their only advantage is a cheapness and hard wearing quality—a kind of uniform for youngsters, but a mistaken concept in my opinion. Corduroys are equally useless for the lightweight man.

Socks are a different decision. Good woollen socks and stockings are best in so many ways as the outer shell of footwear. But they need cossetting when being washed to prevent shrinkage. I often use cheaper nylon towelling socks and discard them when the pile becomes flattened. This way I can wash and dry them easily on the trail. If you do go for woollens, buy the best pre-shrunk nylon reinforced pair you can find. Stockings if you like them, socks if you do not.

Over the feet and under the woollen socks can go any good nylon socks. These will wash easily and dry on the back of your pack as you walk so there is always a change ready for morning and a clean pair to put on tired feet at the midday halt. I suggest three pairs at least.

With double socks not only do you get a better cushion for your feet and allow more airspace for pumping, cooling and venting air around your boots with each step, but any chafing takes place between the layers of socks and not between your foot and the sock. This helps to ward off blisters.

Do not forget to wear both pairs of stockings or socks when you go to buy your boots to ensure a proper fit.

As for spare clothing all that is required is a light pair of washable cotton/polyester trousers or shorts and perhaps a short-sleeved coat-length Viyella shirt. Take extra socks as mentioned and two pairs of underpants—nothing raises morale more quickly than a change of underpants—and a spare T-shirt. Paper underwear would seem to be ideal for the lightweighter. But my experience with this fibrous non-woven material indicates it is too flimsy for the job. In winter, when washing out underwear is impossible, try a pack of five paper underpants and use them as disposable liners to ordinary woven underwear. With a tough outer shell the non-woven material will last through the day and absorb all soiling. Disposal is by burning and five pairs only weigh about 1 ounce.

I have almost forgotten to mention the head. It is a physiological fact that the head is the body's best heat regulator. If you want to be warm quickly cover the head—it is as simple as that. If you are balding like me, you will need head protection against the sun's rays and the keen wind. Do not buy a hat which is impervious—the moisture will not get away and you will suddenly feel cold. Go for a light woollen hat which can be drawn down over the ears in cold weather and worn in your sleeping bag pulled well down if the temperature is freezing outside. Perhaps you can get a friend to knit you one—but buy the wool for it—botany or fine lambswool—otherwise it might irritate your scalp—and ask for it not to be too tight either.

In really cold weather I recommend proper thermal underwear—vest and underpants—made by Damart Thermawear. There is also a special undersuit made by Damart for people who trudge around in the bitter cold of winter and want the best protection from the rudeness of the wind. This rigout is a special polyester fibre and can also be worn in a sleeping bag. But although this thermal underwear is light the more you take along the more weight keeps creeping in the pack.

Two pieces of clothing which I have not mentioned are the belt and gloves. The great Horace Kephart reckoned that braces were superior to belts. In a way he was right. With braces the trouser band need not be tight, and this allows moisture laden warm air to vent to the atmosphere with each stride. A belt restricts this flow. But I prefer a leather belt with properly fixed buckle. And if you use a packframe with waist belt or pelvic harness the advantage of braces is lost anyway.

Plastic belts have a nasty habit of failing just at the wrong time so buy a good leather belt just wide enough to enter the waistband tunnel of your trousers—a narrow belt can be uncomfortable.

Gloves become essential to the walker whenever the temperature dips below 10°C (50°F) and the wind is blowing hard. The hands swing back and forth creating a bigger chill factor than the slower moving body and since these extremities are less well off for blood supply the fingers get uncomfortably cold. Even in summer, in pouring rain, when the march is long, the fingers can get quite chilled. But by drawing the hand up inside the cuff of the cagoule much of the drenching can be eliminated. This action also allows ventilating air to be pumped up and down the sleeve of the cagoule with each swing thus keeping the inside of the cagoule arms freer of moisture.

For winter use and the last cold days of spring I have always used some heavy woollen Austrian mitts. These ***handshuen*** are densely felted and keep out the wind but still allow moisture to be vented out to the atmosphere. A mitt allows finger movement and better warming of the extremities than a true glove.

For really cold weather a pair of silk gloves can be worn inside the woollen mitts.

More about keeping warm—and cool—in chapter 4.

In the section on the cagoule I mentioned a bandanna handkerchief which can be used as a scarf. In case you have forgotten it I will remind you of its virtues: besides being a scarf it can be a head cap, a shield for the face in sandy and dusty country where the wind is blowing, a sling, and at a pinch, a towel.

Paper handkerchiefs can be substituted for cotton pocket handkerchiefs as well as being used as toilet paper. However, there is a lot of comfort in a good cotton handkerchief so perhaps just one is worth its pocket room.

Throughout this section on clothing I have talked of clothing suitable for the male. Intelligent females who are contemplating going light will already have mentally substituted trousers for slacks and added bras to the list. There is nothing else in my considerations which has to be changed to suit a woman.

Women, by virtue of their physiology, are blessed with a deeper layer of fat just under the surface of the skin and, provided the fatless extremities such as feet and fingers, ears and scalp, are well protected, women can stand cold temperatures more easily than men.

As for walking boots, manufacturers have recognized the need for a lighter boot without sacrifice of the essential features. All good stockists keep good women's boots. The rest of the outfit might not sound glamorous but with a sense of colour a woman can outfit herself sensibly from the list I have given without losing her femininity.

As for scents and cosmetics, these can be best left at home—the outdoors will bring out all the natural colours in the skin that cosmetics simulate for urban dwellers imprisoned in the gloom of office buildings or tiny kitchens. Hair styles should be easily managed with a comb and perhaps a small tube of 'Vitapoint' will find pack-room to keep an unruly lock in place.

It is a good idea to keep a tube of glacier crême in the toilet bag to ward off too much sun on the face. A supply of tampons is also essential for comfort in out-of-the-way places—especially when going foreign.

For spare clothing a woman might substitute the light slacks with a denim skirt and coat-length Viyella shirt with a blouse. The choice is purely personal. Tights should be taken for the same reasons I have given for men—insulation and keeping a sleeping bag clean.

A purse, like a wallet, has little use on the trail, but if it makes you feel happier, take a small leather zipper purse to keep the odd bits and pieces in. Then stow it in an outside pocket of your rucksack.

The list of equipment I have now discussed should cover most forms of outdoor living. Beside the needs of the true backpackers there are specialist needs for the cyclist and canoeist. I will discuss these in chapter 8. From the list of equipment we can now draw up tables and weights for various types of travel, beginning first of all with the ultra-lightweighter travelling from hostel to hostel by hitch-hiking:

FEATHERLIGHT KIT	*pounds*	*ounces*
Shoulder bag		14
YHA standard sheet sleeping bag		8
Cagoule		9
Over-trousers or leggings		8
Small towel		7 (dry)
Toilet bag, containing toothpaste, brush, soap, comb		8
Pair of light trousers	1	0
T-shirt, cotton		6
Three pairs nylon socks		4
Three pairs underpants		6
Two pairs woollen socks		7
First aid pack, fly repellent, etc., toilet tissue, J-cloths		9
Knife, can opener, bottle opener		6
Dessert spoon		2
Plastic mug (½ pint)		1½
One pack of Springlow curry or stew (emergency meal)		2
One packet of 'Turblokken' hard tack, pack of 'Dextrasol'		8
Large polythene bivvy bag	1	4
Maps, notebook, YHA list, etc.		6
Total weight carried	9	2½

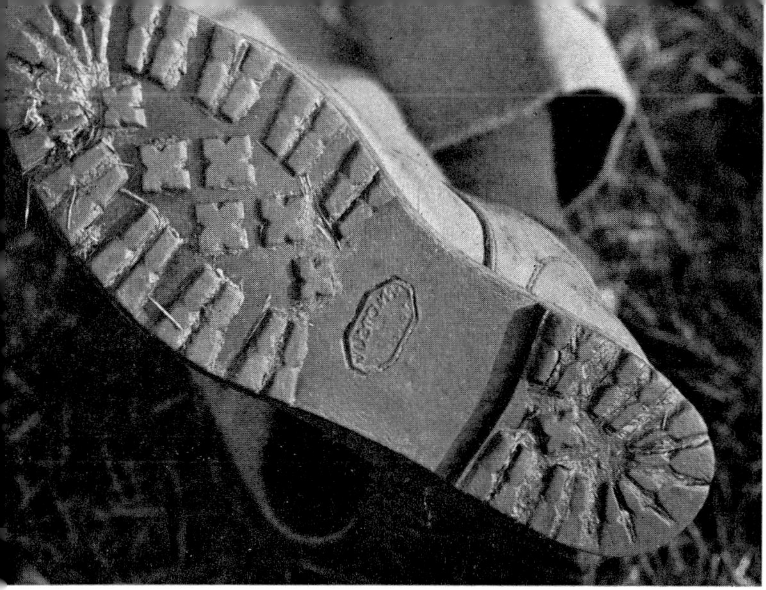

Well loved boots give grip and comfort and years of pleasure . . .

. . . or otherwise they can be sheer hell. Moleskin applied to the warm spot on the foot might just save a blister or total immobilisation

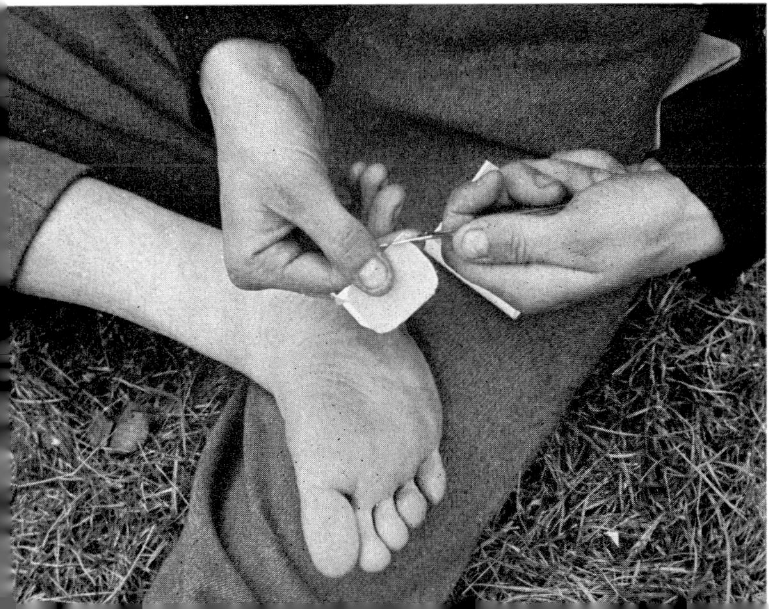

. . . in summer or winter. For really cold work you need protection from excessive condensation, and insulation to lie on the cold earth

Normally worn items:	*pounds*	*ounces*
Woollen shirt	1	6
Boots	4	0
Trousers, wool	1	10
Light wool sweater	1	5
T-shirt, underpants		7
Socks, two pairs		3
Total weight worn	8	11
All-up weight say 18 pounds	17	13½

This outfit is the very minimum weight I have been able to devise to allow maximum freedom for up to two weeks away in an area where there are plenty of Youth Hostels at which there is a certainty of a bed. I have, however, included an emergency meal of dehydrated food and hard tack to sustain a travelling man a long way from a meal.

In case such a lightweighter gets caught out without a bed there is a plastic bivvy bag in which to get some measure of protection on a summer's night in the roadside hedgerow. But the kit is minimal and needs a certain hole-in-the-wall toughness to make it work. It is not recommended for mature people trying backpacking for the first time. More precisely it will suit the student with a shallow purse who wants to travel around in the summer vacation—either at home or abroad in warm or temperate climates. Its total cost should not exceed £20 if use of existing clothing is assumed.

WEEKENDER'S OUTFIT

Like all things involving new skills, one has to learn to walk before running. This outfit is designed to provide the newcomer with the minimum investment kit to give maximum comfort. If backpacking comes naturally the outfit can form the basis of bigger turn-out for longer spells away. If backpacking is not a success then the investment can probably be disposed of with as little financial loss as possible.

The listing is for a solo outfit and totals the maximum load. When two people travel in company the listing can be adjusted to share certain items such as stove, cooking equipment, water carrier, tent, and so on. Although the weights of two-man pieces are obviously greater there is a considerable saving in overall gross loads.

	pounds	*ounces*
Frameless packsack	1	10
Light down sleeping bag	2	4
*Insulated sleeping pad		10
*One/two man tent	3	6
*LPG stove including 6-ounce cartridge	1	4
*Aluminium canteen	1	0
*Bulldog 'Hobo' canteen	1	0
*Collapsible one gallon water carrier		4
*Small towel		8 (dry)
*Toilet bag, including toothpaste, brush, soap, comb, etc.		9
*Small plastic bowl		3
*Maps, notebook, etc.		8
*First aid kit, fly repellent, toilet tissues, J-cloths, washing up kit		10
*Torch (Ever Ready 'Minilight') including spares		5
*Cordage		2
T-shirt cotton, fishnet open weave		5
Pair light trousers	1	0
Two pair nylon socks		3
One pair woollen socks		3
One pair underpants		2
Cagoule		9
Over-trousers or leggings		8
*Knife, can opener, bottle opener, etc.		6
Dessert spoon		2
Plastic mug (one pint)		2
Food: two breakfasts, two evening meals, midday snacks, cooking oil, butter and bread substitutes	1	8
Total weight carried solo	17	3
Add normally worn items as in previous list	8	11
*Shareable items — All up total weight	25	14

Already you can clearly see what I said at the outset. Weight steals into the pack in the blink of an eye. Some saving could be made for weekending during settled weather in high summer. You could sleep out with only a polybag or crude shelter formed by natural materials, but I want you newcomers to backpacking to enjoy your newfound leisure. The hard stuff can be practised later.

The total cost of this outfit should be no more than £50 including the tent and sleeping bag—the two major items of expense. For twosome outfits based on the above list the individual cost is lower. His carried weight should come down to about 15 pounds and hers about 12 pounds.

If weekending is enjoyed, the above list can be stretched to sustain a week away without much more addition other than extra gas canisters, extra food and better washing facilities. Two Primus 2202 canisters for the Tilley stove will be adequate gas for a week away —especially if there is opportunity to build the odd open fire. Food can be calculated at about 1 pound 8 ounces a day per head if everything is carried for the trip. Shopping every third day keeps weight down.

For confirmed campers, who normally go out with a frame tent or caravan for Bank Holiday and annual holidays but also want to travel light, this weekender's outfit, with a few refinements, will be permanent kit. Given care and a make-and-mend every winter, the outfit will last for years.

LONGER-TERM KIT

Finally I will list an outfit suitable for temperate and cold latitudes and wilderness camping for extended periods away from grocery shops and civilized areas. It can also be used for winter camping with some additions.

	pounds	*ounces*
Packframe with pelvic harness	3	7
Plus Stuff sack		6
*Tent: Two/Three man	4	0
Sleeping bag, either down or man-made fibre	3	3
Air mattress	2	6
*Stove: petrol or paraffin	1	10
*Seven days' fuel supply in container	1	9
*Aluminium canteen and extra saucepan	1	5

	pounds	*ounces*
*Two small towels	1	0 (dry)
*Toilet bag, including toothpaste, brush, soap, comb, etc.		12
*Small plastic bowl		3
*Maps, notebooks, etc.	1	0
*First aid kit, fly repellent, toilet tissues, J-cloths, washing up kit	1	2
*Torch (Scout Torch) including spares	1	4
*Cordage		2
*Two sheets of 350 mill polythene 5 by 8 feet		11
Two T-shirts cotton fishnet openweave		10
Pair light trousers	1	0
Three pairs nylon inner socks		5
Two pairs woollen outer socks		6
Two pairs underpants		4
Cagoule		9
Over-trousers or leggings		8
Knife		5
*Bottle can opener, cork lifter		1
Dessert spoon		2
Plastic mug (one pint)		2
Light shoes (moccasins)	1	0
Compass (Silva)		3
Whistle		1
*Collapsible water carrier (one gallon)		4
*Two carriage candles, extra matches, etc.		7
*Small transistorized radio		5
*Small trowel		8
*Folding saw (Rolcut)		7
*Polybottles and food boxes		6
Total weight carried	32	6
Add for cold temperature:		
Down waistcoat		8
Thermal underwear		9
BB sleeping pad		10
Woollen hat		3
	34	4
Food for 14 days at 1 pound 8 ounces day minimum	21	0

*Shareable item

This total weight reduces with each day's intake. Sending on forward luggage to make a cache in the area of travel is obvious.

Add to the main total 8 pounds 11 ounces for items normally worn and we come to the staggering total of 64 pounds! Hardly travelling light, you will say.

But let us consider this total for a moment. Twosome travel will split about 15 pounds between two people, so the carried weight comes down to say 48 pounds. Travel to the wilderness area means weight can be deducted in food/days for the trip in. For example three days to arrive in the chosen area will need only 4½ pounds of food for each person. The rest can be sent on and cached in the local post office, *poste restante*. So now the total load carried comes down to 31 pounds 4 ounces—a much more manageable load and within my maximum limit of 35 pounds.

It must be borne in mind that I have deliberately chosen the worst possible conditions of travelling light, cold temperature and camping in the wilds for up to 14 days. Only the stalwarts will be going to such limits and with a pelvic girdle harness, as fitted to the very best types of packframes, even 55 pounds can be carried without distress for distances of up to say eight miles each day.

Under the list of luxuries I listed a radio, camera and binoculars. Before concluding the section I aught to pass on a few tips about these items which can save some weight.

Let's take the radio first. I used to have a dinky little Russian set no bigger than a deaf-aid which was marvellous. But alas it finally packed up and there are no replacements. I searched in vain. Even tried to make my own on a piece of Veroboard with soldering iron and tiny components from a radio shop. It was a failure—perhaps because I'm not good at seeing tiny things these days. So I came to the cross-roads and said: 'What do I need a radio for anyway?' For two whole seasons I tramped around silently and uninformed; miserable. So I combed the hi-fi shops and tried lots of tiny sets. Eventually I found one that had both long and medium wave-bands on it and it was powered by the standard AA sized (HP7) cell. I demand long wave not so much for Radio Two but for the shipping forecast.

It weighs almost four ounces, but it keeps me happy—remember I walk alone most of my time and I just love my Radio Three and its music, especially on a wild night while I'm making some supper. But AM broadcast band is so susceptible to interference most of my enjoyment is spoiled. Then in Hong Kong I found a really miniature VHF/AM receiver that also worked on AA batteries. It has added a few more ounces, and I'm even happier now. I suppose with age there are things you will put up with even though they are hard work. I am reminded of the great Horace Kephart who had a fondness for a china mug that weighed a ton. But he never went anywhere without it—his weighty bit of luxury in the wilderness. I think *he* was quite old at the time too!

Binoculars need not be heavy. All the leading Japanese optical makers have some skeletal lightweight models in their catalogues and most people cannot handle bigger than 8X anyway. But since I am blind in one eye binoculars are wasted on me. I carry a tiny 8X monocular made before the 1939–45 war for German officers by Leitz. This jewel weighs only four ounces and is very adequate for my purpose—a spot of birdwatching and conning the trail ahead to save having to make a diversion. The same type of monocular is still being made by the British optical maker Wray, and is to be seen in most catalogues.

Finally, a word on cameras. I used to be a professional photojournalist, earning my living by the camera. I have had many cameras from 6X6 twin lens reflexes down to half frame. Because pictures meant money to me I carried two cameras, one for colour and one for mono work. When the half frame system came along some years ago, I fell in love with the Olympus 'Pen F' single-lens reflex with interchangeable lenses. It was no good for professional colour but, my, how that camera worked in mono—some of my best work was done on it. So if you are a serious worker in mono and want to use long focal length lenses look around the shops for a Pen F or the later Pen FT. A standard f1.8 lens, a 16 mm wide angle and a 100 mm tele would be a fine lightweighter's outfit weighing no more than two pounds say. And think of it—72 frames on each roll. Actually you get about 77 frames.

For the snap shooter in mono there are still Olympus Pen EE automatics around in the half frame system. For 35 mm full frame colour try the Olympus 'Trip 35' and the more advanced Olympus 35 ED—both lightweight automatic cameras with simple focusing.

If you want something really simple take a Kodak 'Instamatic'; they are just about fool-proof as well as being lightweight.

But always remember this. Of all the thousands of pictures I have taken in my life—most of them still filed away somewhere—I never look at them nowadays.

More about photography in chapter 9.

The equipment I have listed in this chapter by no means exhausts all that is available for the lightweighter. My list is a personal one of items that I have tested under conditions one finds in the wilderness. Substitute items of your own fancy as you wish, always bearing in mind the basic assumptions we started with at the beginning: Is it light? Is it tough? Can it do more than one job satisfactorily? *Do I really need it?* Then you will not go far wrong.

2

Marching on your stomach

Next to equipment, the most important aspect of travelling light is food. Perhaps I am wrong in this and should have put food first, because you can travel a long way on a fine day without any kit at all, but you will certainly not last the day through without food and drink.

For the sake of tidiness I have put food second in the chapter listing so let's stop quibbling about where it goes and get down to the feeding trough.

Some considerata first: Food will form the biggest share of your out-turn load and dwindle as the trip progresses. Food will keep you going. Food will keep you warm. Food will raise morale when spirits are sinking low. Food is nice—long live food!

But travelling light means you cannot take everything including the kitchen sink. Most foods are a lot of old water and there is no sense in carting unwanted water around. Do you know some butcher's meats are actually 'tumbled' in a machine to make them take up more water so as to improve profits? Scandalous isn't it?

Without refrigeration most foods will spoil in warm weather. Other foods, such as breads and cheeses will grow moulds in a couple of days without storage in a cool aerated place. Canned foods are notoriously heavy for the lightweighter. Preserved foods generally lose their vitamin content when processed. Eggs do not take kindly to rough handling. Fish stinks pretty damn quick. Many biscuits turn to crumbs in half a mile of walking. Butter runs away once the temperature rises above 20°C.

If I go on much longer it will not be worth going light. But cheer up friend, things are not as bad as all that. Nor is there any need to live off bully beef, pemmican and hard tack smothered in tinned jam.

There is one thing to be borne in mind though. Most people eat to live. A smaller proportion live to eat. When you travel light you are, perforce, eating to live. However, should you have a snatch of culinary poetry in your soul you will perhaps give packroom to a tiny box of herbs to turn the daily manna into a minor feast. That's up to you.

Now diet is a notoriously debated and imprecisely understood branch of chemistry. Theoretically, it should be possible to calculate all the right amounts of each food stuff to match each day's requirement of carbohydrates, fats, proteins and essential vitamins. But it is not. People vary so much, and one person can vary from day to day according to his or her body's idiosyncrasies. For instance, travelling light with say 25 pounds on the back covering 2½ miles an hour over medium terrain in English summer weather, one could dictate that a normal person—whatever that means—should need so much protein and so much carbohydrates to remain in fit shape to do the same again tomorrow.

But one can't. And here are some of the reasons why. The night temperature might fall to near freezing, sapping more calories than was allowed for; a touch of 'travellers joy' might mean the gut fails to extract enough food value from the day's intake before it is voided, then the following day out comes the sun in full glory and the body absorbs 300 calories an hour from 93 million miles away in space. The result: lassitude, poor appetite, a cold night, and some heat exhaustion, with an overblown feeling in the stomach.

Dietary needs are a guide only and should be treated this way. Satisfaction, 'stick-to-the-ribs-ability', capricious desire for a certain taste, relish and anticipation all have their parts to play. Pure hunger can quickly be satisfied; steady output of energy in the ensuing hours after a meal is much harder to produce. And all this juggling, remember, must be done on a small stove and with a minimum of pans and dishes.

Firstly, let me clear the board with some essential patterns which must be established so that my plan can be put into action. Whatever you do, DO NOT COOK SOMETHING FOR THE FIRST TIME WHEN YOU ARE OUT IN THE STICKS. This could mean disappointment. Try out all your recipes at home and adjust the ingredients and quantities until you are stove perfect. Then try them out in field conditions on an afternoon hike close to home and see if the formula still works. If it does, write it down carefully for future use.

Secondly, walking is rather different to working in an office. You might just stagger on to that commuter train every working morning with only a cup of instant coffee in your belly and grumble-guts away until lunchtime. But you won't on the trail. You will flop by ten and wish to God it was lunchtime, or worse still, that you had never taken up the idea of backpacking just because some idiot wrote a book about it.

The traveller's day is divided into three dietary parts: breakfast, lunch and supper. Breakfast is the prime meal of the day; the big shot of long-lasting energy to drive you forward with the evaporating dew and the climbing sun. Lunch is stoke-up time to see you on till sundowning. Supper is the tuck-you-up for a sound night's rest to refresh the tired body. In between meals can come minor packets of energy to burst out as the spirits flag. I know of no other satisfactory method of feeding which will allow travelling light to be enjoyed to its full. Only stormy days change the pattern. Days when cooking comes hard and there is only lying in state in the sleeping bag to the unrelenting hammer of driven rain on the roof, which, of course, raises no big appetite for three course meals. Mercifully, such days come infrequently, even in our notorious weather patterns.

So the plan is something like this. Wake with the birds—relieve the pressure on the bladder—and brew the first cup of tea for the day. This can be done from inside the sleeping bag—the tea making I mean—according to your temperament. A hot cuppa first thing in the morning sets you up, gets the kidneys working, and puts some moisture into the system for evaporating off later in the morning to keep the body's heat balance working in tune (see chapter 4).

Have a good wash and set out the sleeping bag for airing then turn to breakfast making. This glorious meal should not be rushed but enjoyed in comfort. Don't crouch, dear, it's bad for the digestion! Set out a piece of polysheeting as a preparation area and breakfast table and put your insulating mat underneath to stop the cold ground striking through to your backside.

Breakfast should consist of a good protein intake, some fat and a fair amount of carbohydrates. Protein will stick with you through the morning and the carbohydrates will release plenty of energy as the sun comes up. Drink copiously and stow your loose gear as the last cuppa cools. Strike camp and shoulder up with a good resounding burp if you can manage one. Try to be on your way by 7.30 or 8 o'clock in the summer months and keep walking until about 11.00. Then stop, throw off your pack and get out the poly-sheeting and ground pad again. Take five bars' rest before making lunch.

Luncheon should restore some energy and top up the water tanks for more evaporation in the afternoon. But luncheon should not be a heavy meal, otherwise you will drop off in the sunshine and it will be 3 o'clock before you surface. I know, my friend, because it happens to me all the time.

Aim to quit walking at the first likely looking campsite after 4 o'clock. Set up camp and make a brew of tea, and a small snack maybe. This will give a hour or so of exploration around camp before it is time to make supper. This evening meal should not be too heavy. You don't sleep well on an overfull stomach. And there are chores to be done after supper, like washing out a pair of socks and underpants while there is water at hand. As twilight sets in you might take another stroll around for ten minutes or so, then a cup of Horlicks or cocoa before hitting the sack. Before you know where you are the birds will be singing again. . . .

Before I turn to specific foods, I must tell you that food taken in a packsack which is cooked but not eaten is not only a waste of food but a waste of weight penalty which has been carried so far. After a few weekend trial trips you should be able to gauge exactly what you need at each mealtime. Try to keep a record of these trial trips so that you can work another important lightweighter's trick —prepacking.

Before each trip you must work out in detail each day's menu and then weigh out on the kitchen scales the exact amounts determined by your previous trial runs. These quantities are then repacked into polybags, twisted up with a piece of wire at the neck after expelling as much air as possible and then clearly marked on the outside with a felt-tip pen—along the bottom seam is a good place—what the bag contains.

As the day's menus are built up, each day's rations are then packed again into a larger polybag together with the etceteras necessary to make up a complete larder for each day. For instance, you will need salt, seasoning, jams, marmalade, bread substitutes and so on. With the exception of the bread substitutes, you can pack all these items into the day's ration bag. Kraft Foods make some very handy things for the lightweighter, such as what they call 'control portions' of jams, salt and freshly ground black pepper in moisture resistant sealed packs, sauces, ketchup and sliced long-life cheese. I have tried them all and I think they are good. You buy them in trays of 20 portions and each contains about an ounce. Any unused portions can go into the next day's ration bag.

Bread substitutes need more careful handling so I pack mine in a 'Tuppaware' box or a snap-on lid polybox bought from Woolworths. I have two main sorts, Crawford's breakfast biscuits and Ry-King. Both are fairly sturdy when separated from other gear. Sometimes I take a foil-wrapped pack of pumpernickel.

I have given up taking butter or margarine on my backpacking trips—firstly it is not easy to carry and secondly it is a sand-trap. So instead I now use 'Primula' cheese spread which comes in tubes weighing 5¼ ounces net. One tube lasts me about three days, comes out fresh with each squeeze and does not need refrigeration. If used from the bottom, the tube can be hacked off with a knife to save weight as the contents are used up. As for taste, it is very difficult to tell the difference between the bland-tasting cheese and English butter when spread over with jam or marmalade, honest!

For cooking, now that I use no butter, I take along a few ounces of cooking oil in a small Green Top polybottle. Another wonderful thing which comes in tubes is Nestlés sweetened condensed milk. A long time ago I began drinking tea and coffee without milk so I rarely need fresh milk. The Nestlés tube satisfies me as a milk substitute, a sweet spread on Ry-King and a spot in a mug of tea when I have guests. It is a dream when squeezed over a pudding course instead of custard.

Of course tea bags were made for lightweighters, but tea quickly picks up taste from other nearby things and spoils, so pack them in an aluminium canister—even plastics taint tea. Reckon on two bags to the pint of tea and then count up your needs for the day. Multiply this total for the days on the trip and you will not be far wrong.

Incidentally, instant coffee is made in one-cup sachets and real freshly ground coffee is sold in bags similar to tea bags. Stow them away from your tea bags if you don't want a strange taste in the morning cuppa.

Cocoa can be weighed out into homemade sachets—negative bags bought from any photographic dealer and sealed up with 'Sellotape'. Fruit drink crystals—choose the ones with a high citrus acid content—can be sacheted in this manner too. Fruit drink crystals make a satisfying cold drink at midday or late in the afternoon when the trail has been hot and dusty.

Before I finally turn to main ingredients, let me take a minute to look at what I call trail snacks. These goodies should be high energy mouthwaterers to lift up sagging spirits. 'Mars' bars are good and not only do they give a vast quantity of energy but they stave off hunger too. Good old-fashioned 'Kendal Mint Cake'—a sort of confection made from sugar fondu and flavoured with mint which mountain men carry around in the kangaroo pockets of their anoraks—is high in energy but not necessarily to everyone's taste. Try some before packing it, you could get addicted.

Health food shops stock some weird confections which are worth sampling and remembering. Many are based on honey and some form of crushed nut so they are just right for the lightweighter's requirements. The 'Fructarian' lunch bars, made from all manner of sweetmeats, might suit you too. Boiled barley sugars also have a place—you are looking for sugars and acceptable tastes.

A shirt pocket confection which is specifically designed for energy production is 'Dextrasol'. These glucose-based tablets come in several flavours and have a slightly fizzy taste to them which refreshes a parched mouth. If you are travelling part of the way in ships or aeroplanes and are susceptible to travel sickness you might find 'Dextrasols' a deterrent to that gagging feeling without having to resort to drugs which make you want to sleep. Short sea crossings to islands and other countries can be quite nasty but if drugs are taken which induce drowsiness there is little inclination to shoulder up and step out after the ferry has docked.

Chewing gum should not be overlooked as a mouth freshener on dusty trails or as a placebo for the smoker when penetrating deep forest where smoking is forbidden. There is no food value in chewing gum and I mention it only as mouth and tooth cleanser. Silly little things like chewing gum discovered in a pocket in the packsack can often raise morale and sagging spirits when conditions are bad.

Dieticians tell us that Mr Average Man needs about 2,000 calories a day in the sub-tropics, lazing around camp on a sunny day in temperate zones or holed up in a sleeping bag because the summer weather is bad. On the march in a temperate zone this demand rises to about 3,500 calories a day with a medium sized load over medium terrain. In winter conditions or hard mountain walking the demand could rise to as much as 5,000 calories a day.

A ten-stone man needs about 80 grammes of protein a day to replenish the ravages of work. People of lesser weight need less, bigger people more. Teenagers and youngsters need much more than their body weight indicates. Excess intake of protein which the body cannot turn into tissue replenishment is converted into heat energy, so it is perhaps better to have a little more protein each day than the basic requirements suggest.

As for vitamins, these essential traces of chemistry are vital to body function, but short spells of deficiency do not matter too much. Deficiency can occur because processed foods usually lack these water-soluble vitamins. Any fresh fruit or tomatoes soon put back the losses and since the body cannot store excess vitamins they are voided each day. If you must worry about vitamins buy some ascorbic acid tablets to give you enough vitamin-C and leave the rest.

Diet should, ideally, consist of about 60 per cent carbohydrates, 20 per cent fats and the rest in proteins. But the body can accept wide variations on this original theme and still function well. So that food selection can be made as close to the ideal as possible I shall now list some common foodstuffs giving their approximate values in calories and proteins:

CARBOHYDRATES	*Calories per ounce*	*Protein Grammes per ounce*
Apples, dried	88	0·4
Apricots, dried	86	1·5
Bananas, dried	89	1·0
Cabbage, dried	91	2·4
Carrots, dried	94	1·4
Cocoa	128	5·8
Dates	89	0·5
Figs	85	1·1

	Calories per ounce	Protein Grammes per ounce
Honey	89	nil
Jams, marmalade	74	0·2
Lentils	98	6·9
Milk chocolate	152	1·6
Muesli	160	5·6
Pasta products	100	3·6
Potato, instant	100	1·2
Prunes	84	0·6
Raisins	84	0·6
Rice	98	2·1
Sultanas	71	0·5
Sugar, brown moist	120	nil
Soy flour	78	11·9
Wheat germ	108	3·6
FATS		
Butter	205	0·2
Corn oil	264	nil
Cashew nuts	170	0·2
Egg, desiccated whole	166	13·5
Lard	250	nil
Peanuts	168	7·5
Peanut butter	173	7·3
PROTEIN		
Bacon, fresh medium fat	120	4·0
Beans, dried	97	6·2
Cheese, natural cheddar	110	6·7
Cheese, processed cheddar	105	6·2
Corned beef, canned	65	6·8
Egg, desiccated whole	166	13·5
Milk, dried skimmed	100	9·9
Muesli	160	5·6
Meat, canned luncheon	76	4·5
Peanuts	168	7·5
Salami	114	9·7
Shrimps, canned	32	6·3

With this working list—to get fuller details you can consult *The Manual of Nutrition* published by HMSO—it should be possible to construct properly balanced menus, we hope.

For instance, based on the 3,500 calories and 80 grammes of protein ideal, with the division into 60 per cent carbohydrates, 20 per cent fats and 20 per cent proteins, a typical breakdown might look like this:

		Calories	*Protein/grammes*
P	3 ounces cheddar	350	20·0
P	4 ounces muesli	640	22·4
F	1 ounce corn oil	260	nil
F	1 ounce dried egg	166	13·5
P	2 ounces dried skimmed milk	200	20·0
C	4 ounces brown sugar	480	nil
C	2 ounces instant potato	200	2·4
C	2 ounces dried apricots	170	3·0
C	3 ounces milk chocolate	450	4·8
C	2 ounces jams	150	0·4
F	1 ounce peanuts	168	7·5
Totals	25 ounces	3,214	94·0

So for a load of 25 ounces we have nearly all the calorie intake, an excess of protein which will convert to carbohydrate, and a balance of approximately 50 per cent carbohydrates, 12½ per cent fats and 37½ per cent protein. Not bad for first try.

Breaking the totals down into meals, breakfast might be the muesli, 1 ounce brown sugar, jams, corn oil, and egg. A lunch stop might take some unlisted soup, an ounce of peanuts, and supper might be a potato and cheese mixture with the apricots to follow. A night cap, using up the milk and sugar, might complete the day. The chocolate would be eaten on the tramp.

Whether this menu turns you on or not does not matter—it was written to demonstrate an ever-present fact, the accretion of weight. Quite clearly then, it is virtually impossible to travel light on less than about 1½ pounds of food each day and still keep in physical trim.

Another fact is emerging, the need for other lightweight versions of familiar foodstuffs such as meat, around which so much of our staple diet revolves.

In Horace Kephart's day he felt it necessary to give long instructions for making pemmican and beef jerky at home before the trip to the backwoods. Beef jerky, so loved by the contemporary American backpacker, can still be made at home and chewed on the trail, but although I rather like the stuff I prefer tc eat the special fruits of science.

Dehydration took the preservation of food a long way. Then came accelerated freeze drying (AFD) and nitrogen preserving. Just round the corner is atomic radiation which can irradiate foods to prevent the bacteria from destroying them. We already have ultra high temperature preservation of milk (UHT) and I think the product is very palatable.

All these methods add cost to the basic foodstuff. AFD foods are more expensive than the dehydrated versions they have replaced. The big advantage is that manufacturers can buy in bulk during times of glut and then release them to the market when the foods are scarce or out of season. AFD foods need no refrigeration and when reconstituted taste tolerably close to the original fresh product, albeit with some sort of chemical smell.

Meats are preserved by AFD. Beef, either sliced off the joint or ground, pork in the shape of chops, bacon cubes, and hamburgers are all available to the American backpacker. Soon they could be available over here. But my experience with AFD steaks is not an unqualified success. Four round steaks in a lightweight can cost far too much. When soaked for half an hour in some special salts made up into a liquid, the meat changes from dry balsa wood in texture to soggy balsa wood. There is a vague taste of beef about it and strangely enough the stuff is quite chewy—far too chewy for meat which costs over £2 a pound. So I do not recommend AFD steaks.

Batchelors and Springlow Sales seem to have had more success with their AFD ground beef. Both these British companies sell a largish catering pack which can be broken up and mixed in with other dry ingredients for evening meals. Unfortunately, once the sealed packet has been broken into, the air starts to reconstitute the contents and they will soon spoil if not eaten within a few days.

Batchelors have a number of dishes already made up with other vegetables and ingredients which are very suitable for small parties travelling light, but there is much too much for one to eat in each pack.

Springlow Sales on the other hand have gone for the single-man catering unit and come up with a number of basic dishes which can be cooked in one pan. Simply add the right amount of water according to instructions and bubble away on the stove for the required time—but follow the directions closely. There is a basic Springlow weekenders pack of two breakfasts and two evening meals. The breakfasts are scrambled egg and cheese, and savoury omelette, and the evening meals are vegetable stew with beef and curried rice with beef. In addition Springlow makes a cheese and onion dish as well as selling a large pack of AFD chicken.

Rather expensive but rather tasty AFD foods are now being imported from Canada by Youth Hostel Association Sales. Made by Freeze-Dry Foods of Oakville, Ontario, these two-man ration packs are three-star dishes on my list. The beef stew is very good and very adequate for two hungry men. Freeze-Dry even make AFD strawberries if you want something crazy.

The whole range of AFD foods is constantly being extended as demand grows and techniques improve. But they will always remain expensive when compared with fresh foods. So perhaps it is best to use partially cured foods bought from a grocer's shop which will last a couple of days or so in the British summer climate and after eating our way through these stocks turn to more costly AFD foods for the last few days of the holiday.

Let's turn to foods which can be bought in any supermarket then. Bacon, of course, comes to mind immediately. Although it does have a fair water content, smoke cured streaky is very tasty, nutritious and will keep for several days without refrigeration in an English summer providing it is kept as cool as possible. Have it cut fairly thick—say number 7 on the machine—and then wrap well in waxed paper and seal it up in aluminium foil. Plan on using it for say two breakfasts and an evening meal during the first three days and all should be well.

Salami is another high protein semi-cured meat which should not spoil for several days if left in the piece.

The tiny 'Fray Bentos' steak and kidney pudding in a lightweight pudding-shaped can is an easy-to-prepare first-night supper and not too arduous to carry for the first day.

Fresh eggs, if carefully wrapped and carried inside the billy can in the canteen, will last for three days—you can get three eggs in a one-pint billy.

A tiny can of shrimps will make a first-class curry for the second night out.

The third supper can be a cheese and potato hash—Halliwell's Fry—with some egg powder mixed in—don't forget a sprinkling of marjoram to make it. This dish is much more tasty than it sounds and it is easy to prepare.

On the fourth night out comes the first of the AFD suppers—say a stew.

The fifth an AFD goulash. The sixth an AFD beef curry. Then it's either home or back to the shops, lads.

For breakfasts I thoroughly recommend a start with muesli, a Swiss-style breakfast cereal. It is much cheaper to mix up your own from kibbled wheat, rolled oats, toasted wheat, flaked rice, seedless raisins, apple flakes, flaked almonds, roasted hazelnuts, skimmed milk powder and soft brown sugar. Divide out your muesli into well-mixed 4-ounce portions and bag them up in polybags. Take one for each day out. Then all you have to do is to add either cold water, fresh milk if some comes handy or hot water on autumn winter days, and then bingo—three or four minutes later there's your appetizing base for a good breakfast.

Bacon comes the first morning as a follow-up to muesli and perhaps three slices of 'Ry-King' pasted with 'Primula' cheese spread and marmalade.

A small pack of smoked frankfurters can be eaten as a follow-up for the second day. I find these poly-wrapped frankfurters don't spoil for a couple of days if buried deep inside the coolest part of the kit. To prepare, either drown in boiling water or slow fry.

Boiled eggs for the third day makes a fair follow-upper. Boil another hard for a lunch stop, while you are about it.

We can finish up the bacon on the fourth morning and then start on the AFD breakfast when the fresh food runs out, which means only two AFD packs for the six-day menu list.

I use soups at midday halts. They are easy to prepare—try Knorr-Swiss and Bergene blocks. Soups top up the water reservoir in a most agreeable way—even in hot weather. For sitting out a stormy day soups are invaluable, since they are about the easiest hot dish a camper can prepare.

Incidentally, once you get the taste for muesli you will find that you will get to hankering after some at lunchtime too, so take along two more 3-ounce helpings as standby lunch food and wet weather fodder that needs no cooking.

As for sweet courses to back up the evening meals, the list of 'instant' puddings available in the supermarket is endless. If there is fresh milk available then the 'Instant Whip' packs will come in handy. Cadbury-Schweppes 'Apple Tree' packs of flavoured AFD apple flakes take no preparation. Just pour on boiling water and leave for a few minutes. Top off with a squeeze of Nestlés milk.

'Mars' bars and milk chocolate, which would be carried for lunch stops and trail snacks, can also be used for a sweet course if the day has been so tiring that the minimum of cooking is contemplated. Who wants to slave over a hot stove all day?

Of course, if there is any opportunity to collect some fresh fruit on the way the value of this natural food, both in vitamin and morale-boosting content, is enormous. But more about living off the country in a moment.

Another little dodge, to ring the changes on the instant potato, is to use 'Potato Chipples'. These proprietary french fries are normally eaten cold as an appetizer or bar-side titbit and weigh very little. When popped into a pan and heated—they have enough fat on them to prevent burning—they make a good substitute for chipped potatoes, especially with a gravy. A normal 1-ounce pack is enough for two helpings when used as an additive to the main meal.

If cooking appeals to your finer senses, you will find many items on the supermarket delicatessen shelves which help the pre-bagging of menus at home. For instance you can buy 'Uncle Ben' long grain American rice—I prefer it to patna—and to this base for curries and risottos you can add apple flakes, curry powders, AFD mushrooms, 'Surprise' peas, AFD beef—probably extended with vegetable protein—dried herbs, onion flakes, crushed sesame seeds, parched indian corn and all manner of stuff. If your supermarket does not have a wide selection in its delicatessen go and poke around the nearest health food shop and you will find all kinds of new and exciting tastes which can be bought in the dried form. Chiltern Herb Farms do up polypacks of prepared rice with additives of tomato, onion, herbs and spices already in them. All that is necessary is a quick boil up and a 20-minute simmer to reduce the water level and thoroughly cook the rice.

In case you have not yet discovered this for yourself, I ought to tell you that all AFD foods taste much better with a longer soaking than the usual few minutes before cooking. It is a good idea to take one of your Green Top polybottles at lunchtime, add the AFD mix for the evening's supper and the right amount of water, seal up securely and pop the bottle back in the pack. The continual sloshing back and forth as you walk through the afternoon will ensure a well distributed and properly soaked mix all ready for cooking when it comes to supper time. The long soaking seems to release the dried out flavours and gets rid of some of the chemical taste of monosodium glutamate which is present in nearly all dried stuffs. Dried fruits, such as apricots and prunes, also respond to this treatment.

As I have said, make sure your one pint drinking mug is scratched on the outside with levels for $\frac{1}{3}$, $\frac{1}{2}$ and $\frac{2}{3}$ pint. This takes away all the hits and misses and disappointments when cooking reconstituted foods in the wilderness.

Whatever you decide to include on your menu, let me say once more, never cook something for the first time when you are out on the trail. Try it at home under ideal conditions first—and where there is alternative food if the result is a failure—prepare the recipe once more in the open under field conditions, and then if it meets with everyone's taste, include it in the standard menu list.

For the first timers I now offer a week-long menu. Weekending needs no special foods because perishables, although weighing more than AFD and dried goods, can be taken for an acceptable weight penalty. Nor is there any need to slavishly follow each day-by-day menu in the right order. Once the day ration bag is made up it should be complete in all detail except for water and beverages, so it can be eaten 'out of turn' according to desire.

DAY ONE

Lunch stop: Soup of the day; chocolate.
Tea break: Chocolate wholemeal biscuit; hot drink.
Supper: Canned steak and kidney pudding; 'Chipples'; fresh fruit. Night cap drink.

DAY TWO

Breakfast: Muesli; bacon; Ry-King and marmalade; hot drink.
Lunch stop: Soup of the day; pumpernickel and jam.
Tea break: Chocolate wholemeal biscuit and hot drink.
Supper: Shrimp curry with savoury rice; 'Mars' bar.
Night cap drink.

DAY THREE

Breakfast: Muesli; smoked frankfurters; Ry-King and marmalade; hot drink.

Lunch stop: Soup of the day; cheese and AFD apple flakes.

Tea break: Ry-King and jam and hot drink.

Supper: Bacon and hash-browned instant potato with mushrooms; 'Instant whip'.

Night cap drink.

DAY FOUR

Breakfast: Muesli; fried or scrambled eggs; Ry-King and marmalade.

Lunch stop: Soup of the day; 'Mars' bar.

Tea break: Chocolate wholemeal biscuit and hot drink.

Supper: Cheese and potato hash with 'Surprise' peas; apple flakes and Nestlés milk.

Night cap drink.

DAY FIVE

Breakfast: Muesli or cornmeal pancakes and bacon; Ry-King and marmalade; hot drink.

Lunch stop: Soup of the day, hard-boiled egg and last of cheese.

Tea break: Ry-King and jam, hot drink.

Supper: AFD beef curry with extra peanuts and raisins; 'Mars' bar.

Night cap drink.

DAY SIX

Breakfast: Muesli; AFD savoury omelette; Ry-King and marmalade; hot drink.

Lunch stop: Soup of the day; apple flakes and Nestlés milk.

Tea break: Chocolate wholemeal biscuit (if there are any left—if not, Ry-King and jam).

Supper: AFD beef stew with 'Surprise' peas or whatever AFD vegetables are left; 'Instant whip' pudding topped with Nestlés milk.

Night cap.

DAY SEVEN

Breakfast: Muesli; AFD scrambled egg and cheese; Ry-King and marmalade; hot drink.

Lunch stop: Soup of the day and small can of brisling on Ry-King or last of pumpernickel.

And here is an emergency rainy-day menu which needs the minimum of preparation and contains less calories:

Breakfast: Muesli, Ry-King and marmalade.
Lunch: Soup of the day.
Supper: Brislings on a raft of instant potato followed by popcorn with brown sugar sauce.

You will see that I have introduced two new items into my food list. Firstly a small can of 'Skipper' brand brislings in tomato sauce. These tasty fish are now packed in a lightweight aluminium can and are my ultimate rations—a sort of goody food which I can look forward to when things get bad and use only at the end of a trip when I am homeward bound. I believe every pack should contain something by way of a treat which, and although it might be expensive in weight penalty, does offer a complete change of taste.

Popcorn is fabulous stuff. Unless you have eaten freshly popped corn you cannot pronounce on it. It is so simple to prepare; put a little cooking oil into a pan with a closed lid and then a small quantity of corn—say as much as you can cup on the palm of your hand—into the pan and set the lid on firmly. Put it on the stove with flame turned fairly well up and stand by for action. After a few moments there is a hesitant 'Pop'. Then suddenly it starts like gunfire and it drowns the hammer of rain on the tent roof. And just as suddenly as it started the popping has to stop. Whip the pan off the heat—it takes about three or four minutes and this just gives time to dissolve some brown sugar in warm water to a thick gooey mess. Now off with the steaming lid of popped corn and drench the white and golden mountain with the sauce and begin eating with fingers—very more-ish, filling and nutritive. Two ounces of pop corn will be adequate for a seven day trip—unless you have children along.

Most Scout shops sell pop corn—ask for 'Planters Shur-pop'. One more emergency food block I have failed to mention—I nearly always keep a block in the pack and take it with me in side trips from a fixed base camp—is 'Turblokken'. This Norwegian-made food is based on the old Red Indian idea of parched corn ground fine. If eaten dry and then washed down with a drink it swells to give a satisfaction, and it releases its energy slowly. The 'Turblokken' pack comes with individual squares of different flavours all wrapped in foil and it keeps indefinitely. I would not say it is a gourmet's dish but it is very palatable, and in a tight squeeze—such as being caught out in the hills overnight or when pinned down in a violent storm—

'Turblokken' has a place.

One of the grandiose dreams which people who go backpacking privately entertain in their minds but never voice in public is the thought of 'living off the country'. It is a bit of romanticism left over from the days when humans just ranged the countryside eating whatever came in view.

Don't laugh at the idea too much because there are varying degrees of living off the country which are quite valuable. For instance, we think nothing of buying fresh milk from farmsteads, or eggs or fruit. This is a form of living off the country and should be considered as such.

Farmhouse foods make good supplementaries to the meals stowed in the pack and should be used every time the opportunity arises. Some dairy farms are shy of selling milk to strangers because their product comes straight from the cow and is not pasteurized. But if you are not worried by the threat of undulant fever and rubbish like that, get yourself a pint of the real stuff whenever you can. There are only two things to remember. Farmsteads rarely keep milk bottles so have your own clean polybottle handy when going in search of milk. Secondly, since the milk is unpasteurized it will grow bacilli very quickly if not consumed immediately. Do not attempt to keep farmstead milk for more than a couple of hours during the summer, then you will not go far wrong.

In the summer time, most village people will be glad to sell or give greenstuffs from their back gardens—countryfolk with the race memory of hard times and always seem to grow far too much for their own needs—so always keep an eye open for supplementaries of this kind. Be prepared to chat for a while in exchange for greenstuffs freely given.

Eggs come where you find them. Countryfolk do not mind selling two or three at a time. In the autumn, there will be wind-fall apples in plenty, but always ask—never go scrumping.

Field mushrooms are good eating IF YOU KNOW WHAT YOU ARE EATING. Never take mushrooms without first considering if they are semi-cultivated. If in doubt about fungi—leave them alone. Read the many illustrated books on the subject before trying these wild delights as food. Better still, go with someone who knows his mushrooms and listen carefully how he identifies them.

Wild fruit of the hedgerow is always good for picking in the late summer. Bilberries, whortleberries and blackberries all make good eating if you do not mind the pips and the cooking.

If you know what you are doing there are herbs in the hedgerow too—but you must know what you are doing.

On the beach there is fishing to be done—you do not need any licence to fish from the sea. Shell fish are good eating if you like shell fish, but again learn how to tell a dead mussel, oyster, winkle or clam from a good one. Otherwise you could suffer from a terrible gripe.

Kebab cookery is just made for open fires with fresh foods and if you are walking past a country butcher's shop with the sure knowledge that you will be able to build a fire in the next few hours let me suggest a few of the recipes for your delight.

Kebab cookery is so simple, and if you take up beach walking it will be fairly easy to practise. Get your fresh victuals from the nearest seaside town and then as you pass further up the uninhabited beach towards your evening halt keep your eyes peeled for a likely looking piece of driftwood. Long sticks of pine—the sort of wood used for cargo spacing or deck cargo wedging—are what you are looking for. And if the grain is knot-free for several inches on one end take out your knife and begin whittling as you walk.

Shave the end down parallel for several inches until you have a skewer about as thick as a diary pencil and finally point the end. Keep this kebab stick handy until you are ready to pitch camp. Select the fireplace, collect the driftwood and get the fire going. Salt-soaked driftwood burns pretty fiercely and swiftly in the sea breeze but it does make good coals. If there is plenty of wood along the high tide line you can afford to be lavish and build a good hot cooking fire bed.

During this time you can brew up on the stove and set up camp —up-wind or otherwise flying sparks might melt a hole through your precious canvas. Then when these chores are done you can begin kebab cookery.

One of my favourite is pork and pineapple kebabs. Assuming you bought pork tenderloin in the last town you passed and asked the butcher to cube the meat into pieces of about one inch—this saves messing about on the beach—now open a small can of pineapple rings. Begin threading the pork cubes and pineapple bits onto the sharpened skewer you have whittled as you walked. Cover all unused food to prevent drifting sand ruining it. Then dribble cooking oil over the loaded kebab stick and you are ready.

Sit up-wind and hold the kebab stick over the red coals—not too close, say 10 inches, or things will burn before they cook. Turn regularly until all sides are cooked evenly. If the meat looks like burning, dribble a little more oil over the string of food.

There is only one way to eat kebab—off the stick! Nibble away as the food cools. If you have carried a few crusty rolls with you to last the evening, brother you have yourself a treat.

Kebabs are what you make them. You can string anything together just so long as you remember that some things cook much more quickly than others and if you put dissimiliar foods side by side you might lose them in the fire. Cheese is a bad example. Apples burn quickly and so do onion quarters unless you keep them basted with a little oil or kebab sauce made from oil and lemon juice.

Steak kebabs are glorious. Bacon and kidney bits alternating with onion quarters are scrumptious. Frankfurters, sausages in skins, ham chunks and chicken pieces all kebab well. Try soaked prunes which have been destoned and wrapped in streaky bacon—mmmm. Need I go on?

If you believe that there is not enough filling food with the kebabs, set some rice to boil before starting kebab cookery and then when ready, drain the rice and sprinkle with cheese pieces and a little lemon juice and tomato purée and cover over. Set by the fire while you cook your kebabs and then draw them off the stick onto the bed of cheese-flavoured rice.

Give me kebabs and you can keep your AFD foods.

After eating, smear a little detergent onto your fingers and walk down to the surf edge with the pots and pans. In minutes you will be washed up and ready for a hot cuppa before bed. And all the while the music of the waves crashes on. Up the beach there is a glow from your fire and a vague outline of the tent against the velvet-blue sky. Yes, beach walking has much to recommend it.

For instance when you can have open fires on the beach you can indulge in aluminium foil cookery in the fire embers. Try this breakfast recipe.

Assuming that you bought a small French loaf the previous day and there is still a rather stale end left of about nine inches in length. Assuming also that you indulged in some fresh butter or bought a few of those small foil wrapped packs from the delicatessen. Now split the bread longways and smear the butter liberally on both sides. Stuff the roll with plenty of cheddar cheese slices and fold the bread back together again. Now wrap the lot carefully in foil and pinch seal the edges. Bury in embers at the dead end of the fire and leave alone while you eat your muesli and make your coffee. Then when everything is ready drag out the blackened silver parcel and remove the hot cheesy crispy roll.

If you do any beach fishing along the way and are lucky enough to land a catch you can cook your fish in foil in the embers too. Just make sure you clean it well by the surf edge after gutting and removing the head. Then paint with oil, season, sprinkle with a few herbs and seal up in foil pinching the seams carefully to ensure no loss of moisture and oil. Bury in hot coal and heap more coals on top. Prod it after about 15 minutes to see if it is cooked. Turn half way, bury in a fresh part of the fire and cover well with hot coals. Serve by carefully opening the foil, removing the main bone and eating it as it lies. A piece of driftwood underneath will save burned knees.

Late in the season when there is sweet corn around you can try rolling an ear of corn—soak it in salted water for say half an hour first—in foil and lacing it with butter and sprinkling with salt. Now pinch it up firmly and leave in the hot coals. After about 10 or 15 minutes it should be fine. In Iran they sear fresh ears of corn over a fierce flame. It is delicious with butter or melted cheese.

All this time I have been considering the solo camper, but when there are two or more, make sure it is well established beforehand who is going to be cook. Those who are not cook help around the kitchen area without actually getting in it—nothing is worse than big boots standing in your cheese fondu just as it is 'coming to nature'.

There will always be water to be fetched, washing up to be done and firewood to be collected if open fire cookery is being practised. Simple rules such as these save bad tempers, because nothing gets more raw in camping than a temper exposed to the pressures of cooking. When cook shouts "Come and get it", make sure you are there promptly for your share. You will only have yourself to blame if there is nothing left when you get back to camp.

On the other hand, if you really are one of those people who only eat to live, make sure you are not picked as cook. The open air generates some lively appetites and enhances flavours and tastes. It would be no good for you to ignore their value when the others in your party were hoping for something really good from your skillet. Incidentally, the man who can cook by the camp fire or over the old Primus stove and turn out a gourmet's dish is everybody's friend. That's the way good cooking gets hold of people.

3

Where shall we go?

Right now. With the gear all bought and the tucker box full, where shall we go?

First of all, hands up all those who have been camping light before! This first section is for beginners and if you old-timers would prefer it, walk along to page 95, brew-up and wait around for us there. Or, you can sit in with us, as you wish.

So you new-comers have bought your equipment, perhaps guided by my window shopping in chapter one, and maybe a bit of your own selection too, and you have laid it all out on the kitchen table and weighed it to make sure there are no ounces which are free-loading. Be ruthless and try and reduce even my totals. If you think you *might* need it, the odds are you will not. So leave it at home. We are only going for one night away from base and not too far away at that, so the lack of something you fancy will not be vital.

I am assuming the weekend looks settled—any one of those fine weekends in May or June. The cold nip has gone at last and the blossom is out. If we get a training weekend in now there is the Spring Holiday weekend to come for another run out—maybe a little further.

The point about having a trial run close to home is two-fold. You do not have to spend a long time getting there and secondly—much more important—if anything fails, does not work properly, or the weather breaks, it is not far to nip for cover. Don't try and be a hero on your first trip out. Unless you take to backpacking easily you could give up disgusted and miss so much.

Unless you live in the centre of London, or Birmingham, it is almost certain that there is a little place which is off the beaten track where you have always wanted to go to and yet, somehow, you have never been there. I am prepared to wager such a spot can be found not more than ten miles from your home—say twenty if you live in London or Birmingham.

Let me give you a few hints, since you are looking so incredulous. Have you a canal or canalized river running near your home? Do you live close by the coast? What about that stretch of heathland just over the next hill? What about that river valley that stretches away from the road not far from the bus stop on the north edge of town? Then there is that Forestry Commission planting over to the east beyond the golf course? I can see you are still wearing a doubtful frown.

Let's assume you have bought an Ordnance Survey sheet in which your town is situated. So we'll look at it together. First of all, let your eye wander out of town along the red main road for say a couple of miles or so. Now what do you see right off to the side not more than five or six miles away? A wiggling blue line—perhaps that is the head of the river that flows through your town. But wait, there is a patch of light green along the northern edge, see? Woodland. Now notice something else, those slender yellow roads which keep cranking right and left? And what happens? They are crossed by some sort of earthworks—probably the track of an old railway or an old canal. Look closer and you will see a faint track of tiny red dots in a long chain—footpaths. Now we are getting somewhere.

Consult any one of the better class campsite guides and see if there is a small recognized farm site in the general area. You don't need one with all mod cons but it will make things happier for you as an introduction and should it come on to rain. If there are none, don't worry, we'll figure something out.

If you have one of those opisometers handy—they are those map measurers with a tiny knurled wheel at the bottom and a dial at the top which measures in inches and centimetres and cost a few pence in plastic or maybe a couple of pounds in metal—run the little wheel which has been set at zero from the point at the bus terminus along the side roads, down to the railway track, onto the track bed and then across the fields where the red dotted line is shown until you reach the woodland and perhaps the campsite on the far side. Read off how far it is. About four or five miles? Just fine.

After an early start with your kit packed up the night previously to save time, just follow your nose along this line. Bus to the terminus, quickly get off the main road and soon you are in another world. Don't try to go too fast—about 2½ miles an hour is fairly good going for your first time out. Take a three-minute breather every twenty minutes or so and look at the view—with your pack off your back—because that is what you came for.

If you have been sweating, it means you have either too many clothes on or you have been going too fast or both. Adjust accordingly until you run nice and cool.

After a couple of hours or so you will have reached your destination. Details about camp-craft are in chapter four, so we won't keep the others waiting around. The point I am trying to make is that our England—and even more so Scotland and Wales—is full of surprising and pleasant out of the way places which are only discovered on foot. Tomorrow, after you have had breakfast and struck camp you might like to take another route homewards so as to arrive in the late afternoon, a weeny bit footsore perhaps, and if you are middle-ageing, the odd twinge here and there. But these are only signs of putting to work some unused human equipment which has been softened with too much vehicular transport. A few weekends away like this and you will have forgotten all the aches and twinges and be ready for going further. OK?

Hello there! Sorry to have been so long, but you know how it is the first time out. Now we have all camped light and we can go on further afield. But where?

Fortunately this densely populated tiny island of ours is rich in places to go. There are about 2,000 miles of canals and canalized river for a start—and that means little-used towpaths and discreet overnight campsites near the water's edge.

There are 10 national parklands covering 5,250 square miles. Most of them are sited not far from heavily populated areas. There are about 400 long distance hikes in wild country—Offa's Dyke, the Pembrokeshire Headlands, Hadrian's wall and the Pennine Way among the most famous.

There are thousands of acres of commons and heathlands scattered all over the southeast. There is rolling downland running right across the south of England, and hundreds of miles of empty beaches just made for walking especially in East Anglia and Northumbria. Above the 1,000 foot contour comes moorland and fell—great country for strenuous hiking—and really wild places. There is plenty of such land in the British Isles which is high grade stuff, and far too exerting for tyros.

For top dogs there is mountain walking and scrambling—but I am not a mountain man, so I can offer no real guidance here. It is interesting to note though that there are more than 270 mountains in Scotland over the 3,000 feet mark and that should be enough for any mountain walker to get through in a lifetime.

Once you have a few nearby weekend miles under your boot soles, you can plan for the Spring holiday weekend and maybe a week in July. The idea is to keep it going as many weekends as possible so that you don't have to keep breaking yourself in each time after intervening months of soft living. My guess is that once you have had the scales wrenched from your eyes after that first weekend you will be away without bidding from me.

Perhaps you will recall what I said about collecting Ordnance sheets in chapter one? Assume you now have two or three of the National Parkland sheets on your shelves. Take one down and begin planning the longer period away in earnest—it's good for a soul tied up in office routine or sales conferences and the like.

What we have to consider is the logistic of a longer trip. Journey to get in the hinterland—how far, especially on a Bank Holiday eve? What supplies will be needed—fuel and food—remember village shops are not likely to stock sophisticated AFD items. Type of weather likely to be experienced in the locality—cold weather clothing or just wet? Distances to be covered—don't over-estimate. Your average is likely to be as low as 2 miles an hour even in mild hill country.

It is very important to remember that every square inch of the British Isles is owned by someone, and just as you would resist a stranger camping in your back garden unbidden, so land owners take a dim view of willy-nilly travellers who do the same on theirs. If you don't want to stay at recognized camp sites you have to be quite sure you will be welcome. Go to the nearest farmhouse in the vicinity of your chosen camping site. Then, wearing a big smile, ask if you can camp overnight at—and here you point to the spot on the map. You will either be told yes or no. The other possibility is that the farmer you are speaking to does not own the ground at the spot where you are pointing on the map and will tell you whom you should contact. Country folk are patient and kindly with people who play the game so it is quite likely that if the owner lives locally the farmer will even ring up the owner on the telephone and seek permission on your behalf. This has happened to me over and over again.

If the owner is an absentee landlord, you will be told about his character, the power of his bailiff and other bits of gossip. From this you draw your own conclusions. But whatever you do, treat the countryside as someone else's sacred property, not scandalously with dropped rubbish like so many stupid town dwellers do when they go out in the country for the day. Generally speaking, isolated countryfolk warm to foreigners who are prepared to do a bit of gossiping. In conversation they can help you greatly.

On the other hand you might get a brusque "Get lost". This is usually an indication that someone has been before you and taken liberties. Simply smile, apologize for your intrusion, and then back off with a kindly "Good day". Politeness might win you a change of heart. Shirtiness on your part does not help anyone.

Try another place over the ridge or down the dale.

Wild camping can be done without too much trouble during a beach walk. The littoral is a sort of no man's land generally owned by Crown Lands and provided you do not make a raging nuisance of yourself the civil servants in Whitehall will take no notice of your passing. There is another advantage to beach walking; there is always somewhere just over the dunes or on top of the cliffs which *is* somewhere. If things get bad or you find the going too much for you then you can opt out and catch a bus to the nearest big centre and a train home.

I can recommend the walk from the North Denes at Great Yarmouth north about and around to Hunstanton. The beach varies between sand, shingle and saltings. It will take you all of five days and you will see but a few people—even at peak holiday times. Water can be obtained at most little seaside hamlets as the cliffs dip down to the sea before rising again. So you will not have to carry a heavy water load far—a quart for during the day and perhaps half a gallon for the last half hour before making camp. The sea will provide your external refreshments of body and also clean your pannikin. Using Dylon you can even wash out your socks in sea water and rinse them finally in precious fresh water. A sea breeze soon dries the socks as they drape tethered to the outside of your pack as you walk.

The Northumbrian coast—although slightly cooler—also provides good walking country. The wide sweep of Cardigan Bay is good walking and starting at Laugharne walking around Pendine, Stepaside, Tenby and on to Freshwater West the trail is very rewarding hard sand and rock. Even the southern side of the Isle of Wight is a splendid Easter holiday walk before the summer crowds get to the island.

The Forestry Commission, after years of stubborn refusal to allow walkers through its acres, has in the last two or three years become much more inviting. Some forests are still closed to the public but many are now open to walkers providing all camping is done at points approved of by the commission. If you like forests get in touch with the commission for an up-to-date list of open forests.

Surrey, Suffolk, Hampshire and Norfolk have many acres of heathland which just invites walking. Just one notch up comes the New Forest which is good for the walker despite the popularity of motor campers at concentrated spots, but don't forget your permit. If you get onto the old railway track at Ringwood and walk towards Brockenhurst you will have about nine miles of undisturbed walking with good camp spots on the way. There is another old track which skirts the Forest running northward from West Moors towards Salisbury. And while you are near Salisbury try the ridge road over Compton Down and past Chiselbury Camp.

Up in Derbyshire they have ripped out one of the most scenic railway lines in England. It is now possible to walk from Matlock right up to Peak Forest on this track bed. You have to go through a few tunnels so take a good torch. But the views you will get are rich and there are good over-night camp spots all along the way.

Old canals are even more empty of people. I have in mind the abandoned line from Oswestry to Newtown in Wales. Then there is the delightful Abergavenny canal in South Wales. Try climbing down from Birmingham to Worcester on the main line for something close to the Midlands. Or the Trent and Mersey from Shardlow to Harecastle Tunnel near Stoke on Trent. Londoners might walk the Kennet and Avon to Bath. All canals have a towpath of sorts, and although the rights of way are restricted, the British Waterways

Board can issue you with a special permit to give you rights of way on all the canals under their jurisdiction.

The point I am trying to make is that before we try the glamorous Pennine Way or the fashionable Offa's Dyke, it is best to get some solid practice in walking with a lightweight kit not too arduously and not too far from civilization but removed enough to make a great difference. Canal towpaths, ridgeway bridle paths, heath trackways, old railway tracks and beaches are nearly all level ground over which to develop a rhythm and perfect a personal style. The underfoot going can be quite rough at times—especially on old rail track beds and forgotten towpaths. This exercises the eye and muscle in co-ordination—the very co-ordination you will need in wilderness places above 1,000 feet—I am assuming that you want to go into wilderness places. I know of many lightweighters who are quite content with the beach or the old railway track, thank you. After you have studied the signs of past eras of transport so that you can spot the engineer by the style of his tunnel mouths or the way he built his flights of locks, noted the grooves worn by so many tow-ropes or rescued forgotten bits of railwayana from the brambles, you too might stick at this. Travelling light is doing your own thing not following the herd because it's fashionable to spend two freezing days on Kinder Scout, or rush from Chepstow to Prestatyn in a week to earn an enamel badge.

As a guide to Britain I would suggest you use Ordnance Survey 'Route Planning' maps, which show the type of country you can study in detail on the relevant one inch scale Ordnance Maps. Select the area in which your town is situated and then scan your detailed maps carefully for good walking country, especially trails which are close at hand. There's no point in driving two hundred miles to spend a weekend on a trail meandering say 30 miles when a good trail of similar length is only a bus ride from your home.

Contrariwise, for those people who live in the heart of a big city, choose an area of your fancy. Make a sally there one long weekend and find yourself a good base campsite to which you can return year after year to enjoy among other things the friendship of some local farmer. Then with only a day sack on your back wander to your heart's content and return at night—perhaps even sleeping out light one settled night high on a hill.

We have a favourite site in the heart of Derbyshire Peakland. We are always welcomed there two or three times a year, and each day we sally forth on foot to savour this glorious county.

Anyone who says he must go abroad "to find something different" I will call a fool to his face. There is plenty that is different right here in our own back garden. Not that I am against going abroad, not at all. Iceland, the Eifel Mountains, the Dutch coast from Den Helder to Scheveningen, the Grand Canal from Dublin to Shannon Harbour and many other places will always be branded in my mind as wonderful country I have travelled through. But I have yet to walk through Kielder Forest, or camp on the lip of the Cauldron Snout. I have always fancied a week solo on an uninhabited Scottish Isle and a tramp along the Antrim Coast. . . .

4

How shall we go?

I am constantly being asked what sort of daily average mileage can a walker reckon on doing. And my answer is, quite truthfully, I don't know. I suspect the questioners are mentally mapping out a route which has to be covered in a limited time and they need reassurance from me that they can walk 10, 15, 20 or whatever miles in each day to keep to schedule.

Forget mileage and think of backpacking as hours spent on the trail. Each man or woman settles down to his or her own pace. Mere miles matter not. What is important is how long it takes to pitch camp, cook a meal, clean up for the night, cook breakfast, attend to the necessary chores, strike camp and be gone again. Allowing for at least nine hours' sleep—more if it can be secured—and adding the time to attend to all the details of camp. Then adding resting time of three minutes every twenty—say 10 minutes to the hour—taking a mid-morning snack break of say twenty minutes and a lunch stop of say one hour, you are left with a number of usable hours for walking. Assuming the sleeping and the camping takes 14 hours of the day, and add another hour for lunch, you are left with nine usable walking hours *less* one hour thirty minutes for rests and another twenty minutes for the morning break—say seven hours.

Again assuming a lot, but if your pace is $2\frac{1}{2}$ miles an hour, and the output of energy is not constant, you *might* cover about 18 miles in a day. On the other hand you might not. Wind, tide, heat, rain, blisters, stomach upset, too much weight, detours and whatnot, all enter into the equation. So all I can say is this. Get as much restful sleep as you can manage. Eat slowly and well, drink plenty, keep your bowels open and your feet in good shape and you will get along fine. Stop worrying about mileage and enjoy the view.

If possible, make every third day a part rest day for sightseeing or just plain old lazing in the sunshine.

The next thing I am being regularly asked is, "What is the maximum load I can carry?" And my answer is simple—as little as possible. That is what travelling light is all about. It might sound unhelpful to the casual questioner, but I suspect there is a worrying mental picture of all those stupid people we have seen by the roadside, bowed of back with the most unsuitable rucksack, from which is dangling everything but the kitchen sink. On the plodding feet are either nailed ex-army boots or baseball slippers, and above is an expanse of quivering white flesh joined near the waist by a flapping pair of grey or brown corduroy shorts and a dangling dirk. Berets usually top the outfit.

It is people like these which drove potential walkers into motor cars.

As I said at the beginning, travelling light is an attitude of mind: a continual question of what can I do without? Nothing would please me more than if you were to find me out and discover for yourself that I had recommended a piece of gear which is a pound heavier than a similar item which *suits you*. Don't follow my suggestions slavishly; explore around for yourself and make up a kit which satisfies you and gives you the maximum comfort and safety for a weight penalty which you are prepared to accept. Each of us is different in personal detail, although our general purpose—that of purging ourselves of the prepackaged, glistering, never-never life we are obliged to endure from Monday to Friday for most of the year—is clear. Once we are away on our own two feet we are free. How we achieve this freedom, and for what particular purpose, matters not.

I can understand worry-warts. I am one of the world's worst. At the start of each trip there are little niggling doubts rising like vapours in my mind as I pack. "Will I get blisters? Will that ankle play me up? Shall I have difficulty getting good water in the middle section of the walk? Am I being selfish or foolish going alone? Have I been too mean with the food? Too liberal with the fuel supply? What about . . ."

Then, when I have shouldered up and hitched down the waistbelt, kissed my loved ones tattybye, waved nonchalantly to the nosy widow opposite who hides imperfectly behind the lace curtains in her front window, and turned the street corner out of sight, the doubts evaporate. The journey I might never properly complete has begun.

Robert Manry, who sailed the tiny *Tinkerbelle* across the Atlantic single-handed said of his voyage that every long journey was rather like life. First there came the birth pangs; then the final painful moment of parturition; the first hesitant and uncertain steps; the youthful exuberance of the rapture of it all; the love-affair of sheer extravagant living superbly done when every new scene, smell and sound is heightened by a newfound confidence; maturing routine; middle-age when chores are done mechanically and margins are pared by long exercised judgment; old age when the end is in sight; then finally it is all over. Only the memory remains somewhere, written perhaps in a diary like an epitaph on a headstone. I know just what Manry meant.

I don't want to give the impression that backpacking for days on end is something which can be done easily. There is a craft to it, full of little habits one acquires by pragmatism and watching others. So now that you have been initiated into the freemasonry of our mystical hobby I can instruct you on some of the craft which you must learn perfectly for yourselves.

Let's begin with feet, since feet are the foundation on which success is built.

You have been to the bootmaker's shop and bought the best you can afford. A judgment of fit can be gained by standing in your prospective boots with your walking socks on and no laces in the eyelets. Shove your feet right forward until your toes touch the inside of the toe caps. Can you get a forefinger down behind the heel? If not there probably is not enough room in the boot. Now lace up. Not too tight to begin with and work more firmly towards the ankle. Can you wiggle your toes easily? Feet go up and down over 2,000 times each mile. If you have bought heavy boots—say a pound overweight—you will pick up and put down a useless ton for each mile walked. It is a sobering thought.

No two feet are the same, try both boots before buying. Explore, also, all over the insole with the tips of your fingers. Is the surface entirely smooth? Is the heel pad securely fixed and free from any excess glue spots? Are all thread ends clipped off? Does the heel-piece grip snugly? Yes? Great. Now we can look at socks.

I alternate between two methods of clothing my feet. Against the accepted rules I often wear a newish, thinner sock inside a thick loopstitch nylon towelling sock. But the fit is perfect and there is no chance of rucking. I take time to sock up, smoothing away any crease or ruck until I am satisfied of a good fit. The same goes with booting up to make sure I have even tension on both bootlaces, starting firmly at first and getting tighter towards the top of the cuff. I don't follow the practice of turning down the outer sock over the cuff of my boot as many hikers and climbers do, nor am I worried by stones. I fancy this practice restricts the free flow of cooling air pumping in and out of my boots with every step.

For a change of socks I alternately wear expensive heavy Swiss wool and nylon loopstitch socks which fill out the space in my boots and feel as if I am walking on a deep pile carpet. Very refreshing at a midday halt or in cold weather, but they do take a longer time to dry.

Every moment I can, I take off my boots, especially during the mid-morning break and at lunch. Blisters are caused by heat generated by friction and it seems sensible, to me at least, to let my feet cool down at every opportunity that arises.

Rubbing alcohol applied night and morning a week before a long trip will toughen up soft town feet sufficiently to begin a long walk. I don't believe in the old remedy of tannic acid baths and stuff like that, but try them if it gives you a more secure feeling.

For the first two or three days out I ease the pace to give my feet time to get used to the new pressure of continuous walking and an extra stone or so of loading on them.

Of course I get blisters like everyone else. But I try to keep them little ones. I worry about my feet something terrible. At the first sign of a twinge, I stop, inspect and take action. Even if I cannot actually see anything I take the early warning signs to heart and apply my magic witch doctoring which must do as much for my sub-consciousness as my feet. The magical mixture is called 'Hirschtalg'—it's German for a brand of clarified deer lard which has been denatured and scented. It comes from Austria and is sold by Robert Lawrie Limited, 54 Seymour Street, London W1H 5WE, for about 30p a $1\frac{1}{2}$-ounce stick. This wonderful lubricant gets into the tortured layers of rubbed skin and greases things up to prevent the layers from squeaking. It even helps to prevent blistered sites from forming fresh blisters on the under layer of the afflicted area.

Then I examine very closely my boots, socks and everywhere to discover what is making the friction. Even a microscopic speck under the right circumstances is enough.

Over the afflicted spot I put a little patch of Dr Scholl's 'Moleskin' and sock up again. If a blister has formed, I flame-sterilize one of my needles—I can always tell which needle it is by the rainbow colours—and prick the blister close to the edge allowing any fluid to drain out before treatment.

Only by strict attention to early warning signs and prompt medication can you hope to prevent yourself going lame. Once lamed from blisters you will be camp-bound for a couple of days while the body repairs the damage. Deep seated blisters might even take a couple of days to work out. Wash the feet daily and take a small polybag containing a quantity of 'Mycil-A' powder along to give them a dusting when they get too hot.

My sincere message to each of you is to pamper your feet as if they were two of the most good-looking virginal daughters a man could ever have.

Going upwards we ought to look at trousers pretty carefully. Turn the pair you intend to use on the trip completely inside out. Now go over all the seams and with a sharp pair of scissors snip out every loose thread, every bit of balled-up and frayed fabric and improperly pinked edge. Pay particular attention to the crotch patch especially where it is tacked to the leg seams. If the patch is very small it will pay you to cut it out and replace it with a piece of soft satinized nylon after chopping away any excess fabric where the four leg seams meet. I find that seat seams have an unhappy way of parting when climbing over gates and stone hedges, so I always hand oversew another seam down the seat with stout nylon thread right on the line of the maker's seam.

Take a close look at the fly zipper for early signs of failure and renew any belt loops or tunnels which look like parting. Take a good look too at the tacking around the bottoms. Nothing is more infuriating first thing in the morning in the restricted space of a small tent if you catch a toe inside a started bottom tacking. By the end of the trip you will be left with an extra, wet, and flapping fringe if you don't take action before you start.

The rest of your underclothing will either be new or well washed.

Paper underwear is almost useless, although it is such a good idea. Ensure comfort in all details before you start on a trip. Buttons should be resewn—even new garments have buttons sewn on by machine which might not be secure. Once started, a button thread will soon fray out and the precious button lost before you know it. A lost button means lost flexibility in the regulation of heat.

Clothed up, I should pass on a gentle word or two about general health. If you are able to walk naturally you should be able to walk on the trail. Such things as haemorrhoids, while not troublesome in everyday living, can be hell on the trail. If you are growing a crop, make sure you take along a little tube of your favourite lotion to prevent irritation ruining your day. Decant a small quantity into a tiny plastic pill bottle. One warning for those who are prone to haemorrhoids—and even those who do not yet know they are—don't do any jumping down from fences or rocks with a full pack on your back. This sort of shock is just the precondition which seems to cause the anal vein to become strained and engorged with blood.

Lung conditions might restrict your movements. Check with your doctor before embarking on travelling light. Heart conditions similarly, although sensible low level flat country walking should be all right.

Walking might seem to increase rheumatism for the first few days but I am told it is beneficial in the long run. Anyway, you will be so tired and achy at first you will not worry about anything except getting into your sleeping bag after filling your belly. If you learn campcraft well you will sleep the sleep of the infant and by the third day the aches and pains should have receded.

Eyesight is vital to you on wilderness and off the highway travel. If you wear spectacles, see your optician and get a pair of metal-framed glasses, like the ones the army used to issue. No one will care about your appearance in the wilds and you will not put an expensive and fragile frame at risk.

Allergies such as hay-fever and asthma are restricting and the drugs normally prescribed to combat them are not conducive to alert physical travel. If you are an allergy sufferer perhaps it is best to write off the whole of the pollen season and restrict your walking to early spring, autumn and winter work. Have a word with your doctor. The same goes for varicose vein sufferers, ask the doc.

Hyper-acidity or bubble-belly is a condition often induced by the stress of modern living. If you suffer, it will erupt on the first or second day out as the tensions of the big trip become manifest. Then the rhythm of travelling eases it away. Take a few antacid tablets and when the last has been chewed up you should be fine until the trip is over.

Bladders seem to get smaller with age. Time was when I could go right through the night without the pressing need to relieve myself. I believe it is quite wrong to limit the intake of fluids the night before to ensure a break-free sleep. The kidneys work best when they are being flushed, I am told. Restricting fluids must put a stress on the kidneys. So I have reconciled myself to the fact that before dawn I shall awake with a problem.

In remote places it is possible to kneel by the tent door and irrigate the night—if you are a man that is. But when there is company you have to be more crafty. Try a half-litre Green Top polybottle as a bedside companion, only mark it clearly with a big P or any other unambiguous device so that it does not get mixed up with the food polybottles. Then you can find relief, hardly leaving the snugness of your sleeping bag, and discreetly dispose of the contents next morning. I get the hysterical urge to call out "Nurse!" in those small hours, for some reason.

This bottle-by-the-bag method works well except in winter when urine will surely freeze by breakfast time. I will leave you to think out a solution for that little problem.

Perhaps while we are talking about one function we might as well talk about the other and then we have sorted out this unmentionable subject once and for all!

Since everyone does it—voiding the bowels I mean—it is necessary to ensure that those who follow our trails are not disgusted or infected. Primitive man, so far as we can make out, took trouble to bury his faeces so as to render his spoor less easily recognizable, and later, when he gathered together for security, to ensure his habitat was congenial as long as the food supply held out. In many ways, travelling light is a reversion to this old habit. Catlike we must scratch and cover in a place not likely to be used by another human—or animal for that matter.

Travelling light means that we shall not be carrying spades and heavy trenching tools so we cannot dig latrines in the best army tradition—nor is there need. Latrines are only necessary when a lot of people are gathered together, or a small group is on one site for a longish period.

You will get into the habit, when making camp, of picking up a reasonable stick in readiness and with your nicely honed knife, sharpening the end into a scratching tool—a flat pointed implement about a foot long. Leave it beside the tent for use. A simple slit about six inches wide and deep and about ten inches long is enough to crouch over in comfort. Toilet paper is carried in the top pocket of the shirt for availability and then, when the job is done, the paper is set alight with a match. Only the charred ash of the paper and the faeces are buried.

The moral of this story is: never pass up a good place, because you never know where the next one will be!

Now let's turn to the problems of keeping warm and keeping cool.

The body is a sort of heat engine. Through the firebox door (the mouth) we shovel fuel (food). It breaks up in the stomach and intestines (the firegrate) to be pumped as energy along the boiler tubes (the arteries) for burning off in the muscles. What you do with the ash is your business.

Now this heat flow is used up in the body's metabolism and excess heat which could blow the boiler is carried away in the form of water vapour vented to the atmosphere by the capillary ducts of the skin. Tiny muscles dilate or contract these capillaries to maintain the body's heat balance of about 98·4° on the Fahrenheit scale. When the temperature of the air is about 20°F below the body temperature the regulation of the heat balance equation is automatic and needs no conscious effort from us.

If the temperature rises to and above blood temperature the moisture vapour then turns into a steady weep of fluid, sweat, which must evaporate in the atmosphere or we die. In sweltering humid conditions, heat stroke—or the inability of the body to rid its excess heat to an environment—is never far away.

If you meet with excessively high temperatures while on the trail, encourage the moisture outflow by wearing only a thin white cotton T-shirt which will act as a wick and also reflect some of the solar heating. Better still, hole-up in the shade and sip water regularly till sundown and then press on a while if you must.

Beaches and riversides are good places to be in hot weather because there is usually a zephyr of wind or even a good breeze caused by the cooler water. And while the meteorological screen temperature might be in the upper nineties you will not feel distressed because the excess heat flow from your body is more efficient in the moving air. Don't neglect solar protection from your head and the nape of the neck though. No point in getting sunstroke even though you might feel comfortably cool—the thermometer is probably standing 15 degrees higher than it actually feels.

But we in Britain rarely have to bother about heat stroke. Coolth is the main deterrent to would-be walkers getting out with their houses on their backs. And yet, if people would only understand what is going on and how best to cope with the situation, they would find the big outdoors a good place to be even in freezing conditions.

We need to go into a bit of science now to unravel the secret of keeping warm, but bear with me and I promise to keep it simple. The first bit I have explained; food is a fuel continually being burned off in the body.

From this metabolism of fuel burning comes the main source of warmth, but not all. Not only is the metabolic rate very variable but it is often supplemented by radiant heat from the sun or a fire. Metabolic conversion varies enormously from about 70 calories an hour for deep sleeping when the body is virtually at its least active, all the way up to more than 500 calories an hour for strenuous work. The by-product of all this energy is water—about 1½ pints a day is lost from the body through simply drying out—not sweating—and some of it goes out through the mouth or nostrils from our lungs. The rest from our body pores.

Sun energy is quite enormous. A naked body on a clear day can absorb up to 230 calories an hour of the sun's heat. In winter or early spring and autumn, this heat gain from the sun is stifled off by clothing so we can only expect 10 per cent of the sun's energy gain. Even so 25 calories an hour can cause minor problems as I will show later.

Heat is lost from the body by several ways, radiation—like a car's radiator; conduction—contact with a cold surface; and convection—a sort of circulation of warm air currents close to the skin which are replaced with cold.

Radiation loss is relatively low and only becomes effective at night when the sky is very clear and the stars look like holes punctured in a black blind when the sun's behind it. To prevent radiation losses all we need to do is to ensure that the temperature of the outer layer of our garments is as close as possible to the air temperature as makes no difference so they cannot radiate heat. I will explain how to do this in a minute.

Conduction, which can cause a big heat loss, is when something cold is in contact with the heat-producing skin. Heat always flows from warm bodies to cold and you can test this by lying on the bare ground even in the most expensive of sleeping bags and feel the heat trickling away underneath you. The insulation of the bag has been compressed to almost nil and now the solid layer that remains is draining the underside of your body of its heat in a bid to warm up the ground beneath your shoulders, buttocks and ankles.

Convection occurs when the thin layer of warm air around our bodies starts warming up the air immediately adjacent and soon the whole lot gets into a dancing, swirling movement carrying away little packets of our precious body warmth. If we can interrupt this whirling action in layers of about one-tenth of an inch thick then the action stops and the heat loss is checked.

Are you still with me so far? Right. Now there is one joker in the pack, evaporation; evaporation of the moisture given off by the body burning its way through the last meal. This moisture has to get through to the atmosphere for evaporating off to the environment otherwise we shall be in the same poor state as exists when the air temperature is higher than blood temperature—heat stroke. Unfortunately, while this is fairly simple when the temperature of the air is pretty high, it is a hoss of another colour when it's cold outside.

Imagine a little packet of moisture vapour quietly hissing out of the skin pores. The first step through the clothing—if it can breathe—is fair enough. Then it enters the next layer, and the next. But already the temperature is dropping with each layer through the influence of the cold of the outer layer of clothing. Comes the dewpoint, that is the moment of truth for any moisture vapour when, according to the volume of water and the level of the temperature, it meets its waterloo—literally. No longer is it moisture vapour but liquid moisture because it has condensed.

The same phenomenon occurs in your kitchen when you are cooking with boiling water. So long as the air temperature is high enough the moisture-laden air can remain unseen and in motion in the room. But just let it back up to the cold kitchen window pane and ker-plonk! It condenses out and rolls down the glass as water again.

Once water forms adjacent to the body the clothes become saturated and then the real trouble starts. Heat is sucked away from the skin by conduction and if you felt chilled before you will believe you are about to catch your deathly now. Probably will too if you cannot right things.

So how shall we be saved? Just a minute, don't be so impatient. We have yet to balance the heat equation so that the remedial measures can be quantified. Let me go back to food for a moment and do some calorie watching. As all diet fanatics know, there is a relationship between certain kinds of food and the amount of calories which they produce. In our everyday office lives languishing in central-heated and air-conditioned comfort, a sedentary job might demand no more than an intake of 2,100 calories before it starts making a layer of unwanted fat. Outdoor living and carrying a pack around quite moderate country will push this demand up considerably—see chapter two. Due to all the factors concerning heat loss which I have just been talking about, cold temperatures outdoors mean bigger calorie intakes to cope with them. The little graph in figure 5 will give you some idea what the relationship is like.

But we shall not be running around barebacked when the thermometer starts sliding below 20°C. Left to its own devices the body would first of all shut down the heat flow from the capillaries and then begin restricting the amount of blood flowing round the body, starving the extremities in a vain bid to keep the vital organs in the trunk working efficiently. Then comes the shivering—a rapid muscular activity which tries to promote a demand for more calories locally—but this ceases when no calories are forthcoming. Finally blood supply is shut right down at the extremities and frost bite quickly follows. Hypothermia sets in when the body can no longer maintain the vital organs at that old 98·4°F. And as the blood temperature begins to sink so death follows in a numb never-never land of fantasy, so I am told. At least exposure victims never seem to die in agony by the look on their faces, and often giggle a lot at the outset.

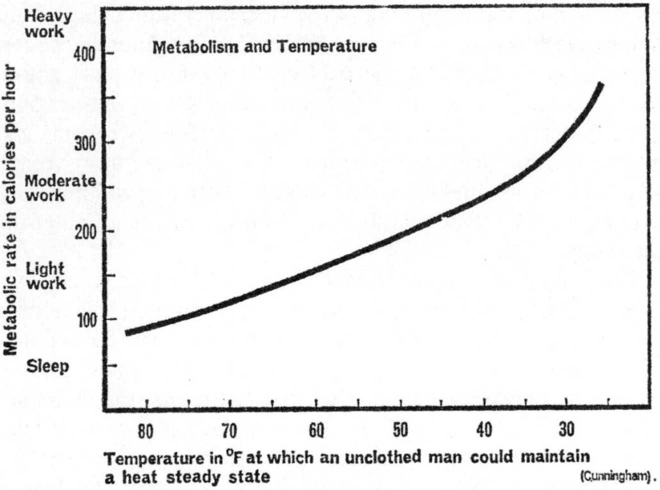

Figure 5

Long before the temperature dips below 16°C we normally reach for clothing and begin wrapping up—higher if there is a wind blowing to produce a bigger chill factor—see figure 21. It is this robing up which is so important and the crux of my sermon.

Remember the layers? The convection currents dancing about? Right then, let's put a stop to them and consider clothing from the inside out. String T-shirts are strange looking garments but particularly vital to the lightweighter. The strings from which the holes are made are about $\frac{1}{8}$ inch thick. And the holes measure about $\frac{3}{8}$ inch square. Being fishnetting, these garments, although unyielding cotton fabric, will stretch skin-tight over any convex body surface. If we put another tightish garment on, such as a lambswool sweater, or if you prefer it, another T-shirt of cotton over the string vest, we produce a series of $\frac{3}{8}$-inch square air cells about $\frac{1}{8}$ of an inch thick. The little air currents are stilled by these cells and they cannot change partners with the next merry little lot adjacent. But we have not impeded the vital outflow of moisture vapour which can 'breathe' its way through the sweater or T-shirt.

Now add another cellular layer over that, and another, and another. Keep on adding until you have reached the thickness of insulation necessary for the activity you intend to undertake. Which brings me to my next little graph—see figure 6 below.

Thickness, as we can see and demonstrate, is the criterion of effective insulation, *provided* that body moisture vapour can ventilate through each layer effectively and there is an infinite variety of control over each layer. Once the body overheats, sweating breaks out. Once sweat forms in the fabric of each layer and eventually soaks right through from the skin, heat will be conducted away rapidly and all the value of insulation will be lost as clothing turns into one big wick drawing away the precious and vital heat produced by a proper diet.

All those which have been skipping this last section can now rejoin the loyal band who have waded along with me through this bit of science. Clothing must resist moisture-logging, be cellular, and be capable of being progressively opened until completely doffed. If there is a strong wind blowing, some of its advantages will be lost and the outer shell should be windproof to prevent excessive cooling of the under layers and dewpoint occurring in under stratas. Wind-

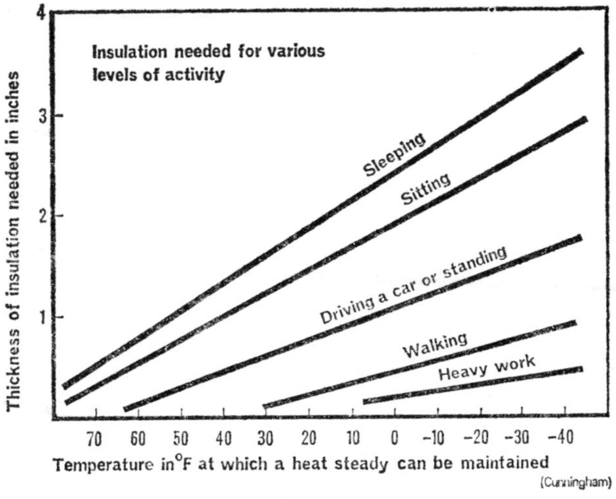

Figure 6

proof often means waterproof—backpackers cannot usually afford the luxury of two garments. So the outer shell is the cagoule and over-trousers.

Moisture vapour, finding its way to the atmosphere will finally arrive at the inside surface of the cagoule and at this point meets its waterloo. Condensation forms and after a time the whole layer is soaking. A little later the outer layer of the insulation is soaking and moisture is gradually wicked back into the inner layers.

Now you see why I said buy a big cagoule with plenty of air space inside it. Air rising from the open skirt bottom will help to disperse some of this moisture through the neckhole, and by swinging the arms with fingers stretching open the cuffs, air is forced up the sleeves. Never raise the skirt up to waist high and draw up the string unless you are descending a hillside and the updraught threatens to balloon you off.

Perhaps you can also see why I never mentioned lots of big heavy woollen sweaters in my clothing list but advocated a down waistcoat instead; sweaters are too inflexible for heat control. Buttoned or zipped garments are best. It should also be obvious why I am so set against the anorak as we have come to know it. While it is a tolerably good windbreaker shell—providing the waist string is not drawn up tight—it is not a waterproof garment and cannot be opened step by step down the front to give flexible ventilation. Strong winter sunshine adds a plus quantity of heat to the body so ventilate accordingly.

Remembering what I said about extremities, keep them well wrapped in windproof material and a heavy insulating layer, because when vaso-constriction sets in—that's the blood vessels being closed down—they will be run a mite short of fuel-laden blood. A well protected trunk however will ensure that extremities are properly pumped up with blood-borne heat.

The neckhole is the weakest part of human design when it comes to keeping warm and clothing designers have never really got to grips with the problem—leaving it to the scarf makers. If you are still cold after robing up with everything you have got in your pack, make sure the neckhole is securely plugged against the escape of warm air by convection.

And finally the head—as I mentioned before—if you want to keep warm cover up the head, the body's natural first-line radiator.

Here is my 5 point plan to keep warm under the worst conditions a backpacker is likely to run into:

1. Cover the head first.
2. Add layer by layer a thick sheath of cellular clothing over the trunk to pump excess heat into the extremities.
3. If it is raining or the cold wind is blowing hard make sure you are wearing a loose-fitting waterproof/windproof shell to prevent rain soaking your insulation or dewpoint occurring deep in the insulation layers.
4. Avoid sweating like the plague. Once you have begun to warm up, start ventilating fast until you reach a balance which is this side of sweating. A change in the gradient or activity will quickly upset this balance—even turning the corner round a bluff or woodside will have a sudden effect on you—so be prepared to ventilate just as quickly to beat sweating before it breaks out.
5. If, after robing up with everything you have got, you still feel cold and are verging on shivering, stop, make camp, cook something hot *from the inside of your sleeping bag* so as to increase your metabolic output and keep straining one muscle against the other while you wait for the hot food. Failure to do so could bring you to exposure collapse—see chapter seven.

Before I close my sermon on keeping warm, I must go back to boots and footwear for just a worthwhile note.

Feet are natural sweat makers—something to do with primitive heat balance systems of the body. Bare feet were able to transfer heat by leaving packets of sweat behind and this left a scent spoor like any other warm-blooded animal. Now that we have put our feet in boots there are problems. Feet carry the body's load which restricts the arterial flow of heat-bringing blood. And feet being the farthest away from the heart only compounds the problem. More often than not, boots are standing in cold moisture—just perfect for conducting away what heat has been able to find its way to the far-flung outposts.

Now you can appreciate why boots made of leather should be able to breathe a little, your socks must be crush resistant and thick to allow plenty of insulation, yet plenty of ventilation. Once they become laden with sweat they become next to useless as insulators. Change immediately.

If you are down to your last clean and dry pair, I'll give you a last ditch tip.

Dig out your supply of polybags and choose two pairs as close to the size of your foot as you can find. Peel off your boots and socks. Wipe the feet with a 'Kleenex' and dust them well with powder before putting on one of the polybags right over the skin. Now put your last pair of dry socks over the polybags and put another polybag over the socks before jumping back into your boots. A good wipe round the inside of your boot with a 'Kleenex' will not do any harm either.

This double vapour barrier method will keep your socks perfectly dry from moisture coming into your boot and sweat leaving your feet. About every three-quarters of an hour you peel off the inner polybag, turn it inside out to dry on the outside of your pack and put another dry bag on your feet after giving them another dusting. The method is not ideal, but it can get you to camp with warm feet and dry socks. Moreover, you will get the shock of your life when you see how much sweat does ooze from your plates.

Cold weather tramping all day can produce a good glow, but once you have stopped, robe up a little more and make camp immediately. Then crawl into your sleeping bag while you cook at the tent door and get closed up for the night as quickly as possible if you want to enjoy a good night's sleep.

Which brings us, at last, to camping craft, the bit that everyone knows how to do.

All day long you have been tramping along looking for that idyllic spot with a lone pine, a burbling stream, blue hills yonder and not a soul around. Forget it. Such spots only exist on American camp outfitters' catalogues and Dixon's carefully manicured picture postcards of Scotland.

By six o'clock in summer, an hour earlier in autumn or spring and two hours earlier in winter, you should have found a level spot, not in a hollow, with shelter on the side of the prevailing wind, and water not far away. Finding this more mundane combination will be bad enough, never mind the lone pine and blue hill stuff. If the level spot is well-drained and has good holding ground for your tent pegs you are really in luck. The site could be a wilderness place or a recognized registered site. Whichever you fancy, do not pass a good site up because there are others sharing it with you. These over-crowded islands of ours will mean that you must come into contact with other humans quite often so don't spend a miserable night looking for the impossible when the suitable is available at some small cost to your *id*. After all, you will probably be away before the other lay-a-beds are up in the morning.

A level spot is a must if you are to have a reasonably comfortable night. No man can lie a night through with his head downhill, although there are many first-timers every year. A side slope will give you a shallow sleep full of dreams of a fight back against the roll and a following day full of aches as muscles which braced you through the night complain for the lack of sleep. Toes-down sleeping gives throbbing feet, insecurity and a bad temper.

So it's a level site every time for me, folks, and it's always my first priority.

My tentage is good and I can stand up to big winds *if I have to*. But I don't go looking for exposure if I can find a lee. Look where the sun is going down, and unless the wind is contrariwise, that is where our British weather comes from. Southwesterly shelter makes sense. The exception to this rule is if we are in the middle of a northeasterly gale which will veer during the night.

I have put the availability of water last, because although it is very important, a level site and proximity to water—either from a standpipe, cottage tap or high mountain stream—might not go hand-in-hand. Given a choice it is the level site and a walk for the water every time. Incidentally, be very wary about natural water supplies, they are probably polluted. Only mountain-top water could be good, and I would have doubts about that. If you are obliged to use stream water or spring water look to the vegetation around and for water boatmen swimming on it. If the water supports natural life it could be acceptable. Make sure with a purifying tablet. Only take running water when you have explored a good way upstream. There might be a dead sheep in it or a cottage might dump its sewage into the water course. Unused wells are suspect.

Now there are level sites and level sites. Many level sites are water meadows in a hollow or hard rock pans. Some are just sand without vegetation. Shun the water meadow, if the temperature drops during a cloudless night you will wake up frozen and wreathed in mist. The same goes for hollows. This is caused by night drainage of cold air from higher ground after the local warm air has risen to embrace the cloudless sky and the stars—our old enemy radiation again. If you can find a level spot just down from the brow of the higher ground to the southwest, you are in luck; a lee and probably five degrees' extra warmth during the night. Rain water collects in hollows if you get a flash summer storm. Rock pan is not too bad if there is a good lee. The warm rocks will give up some of their heat to you during the night and by rigging extra lines from your collection of cordage you should be able to find some holding ground in the cracks or around boulders too big to move. Weight out the tent floor on the inside with four largish smooth stones if you can't drive ground cloth pegs. Sand is fairly easy stuff to use for one night stands in settled weather. Instead of trying to drive pegs, out with your polybags, fill up enough to match all your guylines and soak the contents with water before tying them up with the guyline removed from the tent and reversed so that the runner is working away from the tent not towards it. Now bury the wet sandbags fairly deep and pour more water over the spot. You will not be bothered with the tent shifting but you will get shifting sand into everything you wear, eat and sleep in.

Trees are something I treat with great suspicion unless they are conifers. Firstly, trees have a nasty lethal habit of shedding limbs in the night when the temperature drops; the resinous droppings of the conifer don't do nylon tentage much good either. A good hedge-bottom is much better than a small clearing or a firebreak in the forest. Forests are creaky, swishy, noisy places even in a force 4 when you would hardly notice the wind under a good lee in the open. Trees gather up insects as cities gather up people. If you are running from the city you certainly will not like sharing your open-air freedom with millions of things that go Zzzz all night and day. Better to stop in the city where you understand the things which go Zzzz all night.

Colin Fletcher, *The Man Who Walked Through Time*, reckoned he only once used his compass to get out of danger. The rest of the time he uses it to site camp with. At each daybreak he sights his compass on the rising sun and notes the bearing. Then next evening when he is looking for a place to pitch he whips out the compass and checks the morning's up-sun line of sight. If there are obstructions he presses on until he can lay out his tent or bivouac to get the first light and its heart-warming rays.

When you have camped on the wrong side of a valley mistakenly basking in the evening sun and then sat shivering in the next morning's frosty air awaiting the golden light and warmth inching down the hillside opposite you will see why Fletcher has a pretty good idea.

OK, then, fellas. We have got a level site, a lee, no hollows, no trees, and water is not too far away—in fact only a field or so away. What next, O Great Eagle?

Off with your pack, chaps, and then fling yourself down on the ground just on the spot you have chosen for the tent. Feel around. Any big lumps, hollows, stones, pine cones, ants' nests or other obstruction? Go over the ground thoroughly on your hands and knees and make really sure, especially if the grass is longish. Kick a small depression for your hip if you like comfort.

This rather ungainly search will repay you handsomely later. Now up with your tent, tail to the wind. Smoothly peg out the ground cloth first, joint the poles and push up the spread. Set out the main guys and adjust before you go any further. Look inside the tent and see that you got the ground cloth square with no diagonal pulls or folds. When you are satisfied so far, proceed with the remaining guys, until you have a nice set.

Slide the insulating mat under the ground cloth in exactly the position where you will sleep. Out comes the sleeping bag to be given a vigorous shaking to fluff it up before laying over the right spot. Fold the mouth over and it will not collect insects.

Now off boots, on moccasins. Out stove, cooking pots and on with the pint of water you have carried so far, if you have been walking through waterless country. A brew is the best thing a weary traveller can fix. Supper will be some time yet so no harm in a quick chocolate wholemeal biscuit.

A brew-up done and energy seeping back, now is the time to fetch water and rinse out socks for morning. The rest of the time is your own until supper when cook should remember to work backwards from at least half an hour before dusk to begin preparing food at the right time. Supper eaten, pannikins washed up, pop on your duvet waistcoat and come a gentle stroll with me as the twilight falls. And then to bed.

Hey! Not so quick. There are things to be done if your night in the bag is to be comfortable and restful.

Just harking back for a moment to all that water vapour given off by the body, consider what will happen during the night as your sleeping body gives off another ½ pint or so. Much of it will collect as condensation on the inside of the roof panel of your tent and quite a large amount will migrate all over everywhere and settle. If the surface is cool it will condense. If it is clothing it will creep into the fibres and be there waiting for you next morning.

It is a good camper's rule that he never climbs into his sleeping bag with his day clothes on except in an emergency. If day clothes are left around in the tent without protection they will soak up a fair amount of that floating body moisture. Make it a habit then to stow all your day clothing into a large polybag or the sleeping-bag stuff sack. Then if you find your head is too low, this waterproofed package will perform as a good bolster for your head. Tomorrow you will not don damp clothing.

Unless you need privacy, or the weather is bad, there is no reason to zip up your small tent to shut out the outdoors. Keep the flyscreen closed—every good tent should have good flyscreening—and leave the main doors open. Enjoy the air you have come for instead of breathing recirculated air that your body has used a couple of times already. If the temperature becomes too low in the night a flick of the wrist will close you in.

I put air mattresses on my list of luxuries, but I will readily admit I indulge in one as a utility item and consider the extra 2 pounds worthwhile. The comfort it brings is worth the penalty—at least it is in the morning; I am not quite so sure sometimes at the end of a long day on the trudge when the wind has been against me. Air mattresses have got themselves a bad name for chilling the sleeper because users fail to understand some of the principles which I detailed earlier. An air mattress is a series of large open air cells, perhaps 2 inches thick when supporting a sleeper's weight. The down under the sleeping bag is compressed to less than a quarter of an inch and so virtually all insulation is lost under the pressure spots. The squishy, form-hugging characteristics of an air mattress worsens the loss of insulation by pushing hard on body areas where no pressure normally occurs. So conduction is induced over a wide area. Heat flows through the squashed down, through the fabric of the air mattress, and begins to heat up the air in the tubes. Dancing movements of body-heated air accelerate the process by convection.

Further wriggles of the sleeping body ensure good mixing of the air in the tubes and, before you know it, vital body heat has been conducted away to the ground through the underside of the mattress. The symptoms are a chilly awakening about three in the morning with the spine feeling like an ice block. Examination of the mattress would reveal a damp patch where the body has been lying—hence the erroneous assumption that air mattresses 'sweat', thus causing the chilling. Of course the collected moisture helps the chilling process, but it is not the cause of it.

I satisfactorily solved the problem some time ago during a long dark chilly autumn night. By midnight I was awake with the clams. Turning round inside my bag so as to bring the fluffy upper side underneath me did not help much. Then I wrapped my heavy wool shirt around the mattress and buttoned it up, stuffing the inside-out arms down in the spaces between the airbed reeds. I slept without further trouble. And the shirt being normal outerwear had an opportunity to air properly next morning without damping down my under-layers.

If you see me now, puffing up my air mattress, watch me dress it up in a woollen shirt before I go to bed and don't grin, I am just putting some insulation between me and the pesky air currents. A layer of newspaper underneath the mattress also helps a great deal.

The last thing I do before turning in is to put the cooking stove handy by the door and the pannikin ready with a charge of water in it for my morning cuppa and cover the lot with a piece of polythene. Next morning I enjoy a hot cup of tea in bed without rising.

In summer I rise early and race through cooking, washing up and loading in the shortest possible time to get on the trail as early as I can. It is an invariable rule I have—which I usually manage to break every morning. Lying in my sleeping bag is sheer heaven for me and the precious early morning hours dribble away without effort.

When I am using my air mattress I can bring things to a head by jerking out the plugs and subsiding to the hard ground—which is enough to make anyone get up. Once up I get righteous and revel in the sharpness of the clean morning air and thank my old tutor and Colin Fletcher that I learned my compass work sufficiently to sight the sun-up properly and grab the warming slanted rays twinkling in the grass. Of course on bad weather days, if I decided to hole up—I stay put and sleep on. The morning cuppa warms the heart and the faithful P-bottle is handy to prolong my time in the sack. From under the flysheet I try to discern the signs in the sky and estimate when an improvement will set in. Only hunger gets me up on bad mornings. I travel light for pleasure not for an endurance test. If sleeping on is called for, I sleep on and charge up the batteries.

I quite forgot to mention bed-time for the faithful old boots. Give them a chance to recover for another day when you go to bed by giving them a wipe out with a J-cloth or a paper handkerchief and then stand them where the air currents can get at them and the dew and rain cannot. Undo the lacings right down and pull back the tongue to promote as much airing as they can get. It will pay-off the following day. My faithful little 'Minilight' is my bedside companion, always stowed in the same position for instant use. Unbeknown to me it always goes off a-walking while I sleep and I can never find the damn thing when I need it. I must remind myself to tether it to somewhere, or at least pop it in my moccasins where it will not migrate. As for a sniffle in the night, then I have got a rule for that too. I stuff a paper handkerchief down the front of my tights ready for instant use and, half-awake, I forget where I have put it—well for a second or so.

On hot summer nights I use my big airy tent, unzip all the openings and lie there in comfort behind the flyscreening in a cool drift of air as the nasties crawl all around outside looking for an opening to come and get me. Of course, I might be better off sleeping in a bivouac of a plastic tarp slung between trees protected from beasties, inside a mosquito net rigged up on sticks cut from the hedgerow. But that seems too much trouble to me when I have a good all-purpose tent.

Whatever you do, make sure your night is as comfortable, as warm and as pleasurable as you can make it. Sleep on if you feel like it—especially on bad days and rest days. Sleep is a great, cheap restorer of the body.

Since this is a book which is mostly concerned with walking around with a pack on one's back, I suppose I ought to give a little campfire chat about walking; pass on some hidden mystery to would-be travellers which then makes it all easy. Forget it. Walking is something we learn to do at a very early age and nothing I could tell you would materially change the way you walk at present. I can think of no formula for walking, which, if slavishly followed, would turn your daily average of say ten miles into twenty.

There are some obvious details which help to make life on two feet more pleasurable. I have already told you that I get my boots off at the first halt which promises to be lengthy. I am convinced that this helps me, but it might not help you—people are so different. Scrupulous foot hygiene is obvious, but surprisingly neglected by so many. Sure-footedness with a pack on the back is mandatory if you do not want an incapacitating turned or broken ankle. So always look where you are putting your feet if the going is not hard road or a level pathway. If you want to admire the view don't try and do it while you are walking otherwise you could end up head over tea-kettle down in a ditch. Stop a moment and take a breather—there's no hurry.

And talking of hurrying, if you find conversation difficult and you are short of breath, you are going too fast. Never carry on up a hill if you are feeling swimheaded. Ease off or stop and get your second wind. Rhythm is what you are after. Get into a rhythm which suits you and keep to it—never mind the others in the party. Keep this rhythm and shorten your step accordingly when ascending hills. A steady old one-two of only inches at a time is far better to my mind than bursts of stretching, turning and leaping. You are likely to get there just as fast as the hares who are calling you a tortoise.

On a long march, I am sure there is an advantage in the old campaign walker's trick of kicking slightly at the forward travel of each stride as the foot prepares to land on the ground. An inch on each stride means, theoretically at least, that you have gained about 160 feet in every mile. But it takes conscious effort to make this little kick and if you cannot keep your mind on it you will be back to your normal life-long walking habit immediately.

Of course, those who walk with toes pointing outwards—and I am one of them—do not get on quite so well as those with neat strides of correct stance. We roll off the side of our big toe pads and this can be quite uncomfortable for the first day out. But we toe-splayers rarely trip over things because the triangular footing seems more sure.

My advice to you people who have grown soft by too much riding around in motor cars is this, walk the way that is most comfortable to you, and don't adopt any fancy Olympic styles. Just get a good rhythm and keep it up. A pack frame leaves both hands free—unlike the old-fashioned framed rucksack which always needed hands holding on the straps to ease the load. So swing your arms naturally and if your hands get a bit puffy, stop and take a breather with your pack off. If you are crossing difficult plank bridges over streams or gulleys, take your pack off and hold it in one hand low down to keep the centre of gravity as low as possible. Should you fall you will not be likely to land awkwardly with a pack impeding your natural inclination to right yourself.

There is another question which has to be considered: to travel in solitary solace or in gregarious groups? If you are sure you can stand your own company and the clutch of loneliness is not going to spoil your pleasure, by all means travel alone with two or three provisions. Never go into the mountains alone. Do not go alone to places where you might be putting yourself at risk, and always leave an itinerary with a responsible person. Keep to this itinerary, more or less, and never decide to stay a day or so over the time you said you would. Break cover on time and give a telephone call to the itinerary holder to let him know your extra plans. Failure to follow this simple rule can cause no end of worry and might even bring search parties out looking for you and putting other lives at needless risk. It also gets lightweight travellers a bad name—remember, the newspapers will blow it out of all proportion to make a 'good' story.

If a plane does seem to be searching for you and flies low overhead a couple of times wave your right arm above your head slowly and the pilot will know all is well. He will waggle wings in acknowledgement.

Group travel has some advantages and an equal number of drawbacks. The biggest advantage is load-sharing of communal items. The tent, stove, cooking pots, washing equipment, emergency kit, water carrier and fuel supplies can be shared by and among the party. A group also makes camp chores that much easier, one cook, one general factotum, one water-fetcher, and so on. The problems of group travel come with speed of travel and decisions. Everyone walks at a slightly different rate which can make a party straggle. Twosomes are good, but threesomes can end in rows—two of the three will gravitate towards each other's company, leaving the other fellow outside of conversation and decision-making. Foursomes usually break down into two groups of two. Bigger parties get very unhandy and allow the shirkers more opportunity to shirk. Keep parties small.

Twosomes were made for newlyweds. Everything they will see around them—when they actually see things around them—will be that much finer. Young love is great for sharpening the awareness of life. I do not recommend double sleeping bags except in very good settled summer weather—they let in too much draught down the middle of the sleeping bodies—when it comes to sleeping time.

Twosomes are fine for middle-aged couples. There is a certain drollery which comes from familiar lifelong affection and this can be enjoyed to the full in the big outdoors. Silence for long periods on end is not misconstrued by couples who have lived together in houses for years, so there is no uneasiness. Tiffs and spats soon forgotten.

Foursomes are often necessary when the family goes backpacking. Each child has a preferred parent and the group then tends to split into two groups with a child and parent in each. The fun comes with the interchange of ideas and rivalry between groups. I can recommend family lightweighting. But do take some lightweight pastime along—like a miniature pack of playing cards, or Happy Families. Children get impatient in bad weather and need jollying. Tell stories and make up new games which don't need paper and pencils. An inflatable vinyl beach ball is good to use up excess childish energy and weighs little to transport.

Incidentally, don't mollycoddle children in camp. They are tough little animals and will revel in their newfound adventure, eat like horses and sleep like angels—well, most of the time. Just keep them away from fire and sharp knives. Make it a rule that feet are never bare, all camp chores are shared, and habits clean.

Speaking of chores, let's look at firemaking. The open fire is getting to be a luxury, and in some places expressly forbidden. Never break this order, it has been made for a good reason.

But whenever possible, always use an open woodfire so that you become skilled. Not only will an open fire save previous liquid or gas fuel, but it will open up a wider range of cooking ideas.

Fires come in two sorts, big ones for drying clothes and being generally cheerful indulgences, and little ones for cooking. I have no need to tell you about big fires because that is what most people tend to make anyway. A big fire is limited only by the supply of fuel and how far it has to be dragged and chopped up.

Cooking fires are much more sophisticated. You do not want one calorie more heat than is necessary and, what is more important, you want to be able to get close to cook successfully. Everyone has the inborn idea of making a little wigwam of fingersized sticks and a loose heart of dry stuff under. One match, Boy Scout fashion, and the fire is away. Use windproof flamers to make sure, but only when you are quite certain the fire will take off.

A long fire is best for cooking, and by long, I mean long enough to supply heat for all the kettles and pannikins to be used in a row. The fire should be end on to the wind to give a hot spot for fast boiling and frying and the down wind end for steady heat on hot coals which have been moved along from the upwind end. Two bed logs about three inches in diameter will help keep the fire together and prevent heat loss as well as providing a firm base for the cooking pots. Alternatively you can use a dingle stick—a spiky small branch housed hard into the ground at one end, propped over a fulcrum of a smaller stick to prevent the top from sinking, and leaned over the fire to give alternative perches for the wire bails of your cooking pots. The dingle stick is fine for fast boiling because it prevents the coals being doused by the cold pots settling on them.

Fresh bread substitutes and meats can be baked in camp over a woodfire using aluminium kitchen foil and sticks to make a reflector and the plate from the canteen as an oven 'shelf'. The heat comes to the bottom naturally and is also reflected from the foil to bake a golden crust on top.

Kebabs, meats and vegetables spiked on thinly shaved long sticks are ideal alternative methods of cooking food without pans. My family loves kebab cookery.

Wood fuels come where you find them. On beaches unfrequented by holiday-makers, there is plenty of fuel—usually tar-soaked these days. In meadowland and near woods you can find enough fallen branches and dead wood to keep you supplied for cooking. Don't be foolish and break off living timber. It does not burn and it can damage the tree thus bringing us all into disrepute.

Forestry sites are not the places for open fires—use your stove. Above the treeline fuels are hard to find and stoves become necessary. But where wood is available, get to know what an ash tree looks like and use the wood that has fallen from it—it's the best you can get. Hardwoods such as oak and holly and beech are also good slow burners. Conifers are fast burning and a bit spitty. Elm, willow and chestnut are useless.

Most of your camping will be done when the leaves are on the trees, so I suggest you get hold of a good tree identification book, such as Methuen's *Trees and Bushes in Wood and Hedgerow* by Vedel and Lange. Comparing the growths with my little list of woods should get you sight perfect for the best fuels when you are out in the sticks. Once you have begun to recognize trees with their leaves on you should have no difficulty in making the correct pickup in the winter.

Alder:	quite useless for firemaking
Apple:	burns well once alight and gives off a sweet smell
Ash:	the best fuel you can find
Beech:	second only to ash for a good cooking fuel; burns bright, green or dry
Birch:	easy firelighter but swift burner; use paper bark as tinder in wet conditions
Cherry:	another sweet burner
Chestnut:	forget it
Driftwood:	comes in all shapes and sorts, usually soaked in tar; burns reasonably well
Elder:	will burn well but gives off terrible eye-watering smoke
Elm:	fit only for coffins
Hawthorn:	needs a gallon of paraffin to start it
Hazel:	much the same
Holly:	a fat fuel which burns fiercely green or dry
Hornbeam:	a good burner but will break your ankle if you try jumping on branches for handy pieces
Lime:	once going keeps burning
Maple:	see lime
Oak:	a good steady burner for long simmering jobs
Plane:	see lime

Sycamore:	see lime
Willow:	saturated in water
Yew:	hard to start but another long slow burner

All conifers burn fast and well. Larch is rather stringy and like wellingtonia it will split abominally.

If the weather has been wet, look for dead wood still attached to living trees. This is usually well drained and will burn with a bit of persuasion. NEVER take living branches from living trees.

Firemaking is easy. The uppermost thought in your mind must be to control it and extinguish it fully when its usefulness is done. For a small long fire for cooking try to find a patch of clear earth on which to make your fire. Alternatively, dig out a sod of turf and make the fire on open ground. Avoid any mulches of pine needles or leaves—once thoroughly warmed up these fire beds become dangerous. On beaches, keep away from shingle for firemaking, flints have a nasty habit of flying with an explosive bang. Shaly rocks and limestone have similar nasty habits.

NEVER leave a fire unattended for more than a couple of minutes. And when you have finished with its purpose, douse the embers until the steam subsides, then rake over the ashes and douse again before replacing the sod. Now give a final watering. You can never be too sure. Scatter the unburned sticks in the hedgerow so as to leave a tidy patch.

Open fires are great for burning up all the rubbish you have in your pack. Any food can should be thoroughly burned until all the protective tinning has gone. Then it should be flattened and discreetly hidden in the bottom of a hedgerow—in a burned state it will rust away in months without causing pollution. If in doubt take it home with you or to a point where it can be properly deposited. Aluminium foils, from around food packs, will not break down by atmospheric oxidizing. When you have burned off foils, rake them out of the embers and when cool crush into small balls for taking home. Plastics burn fairly easily with a dense sooty smoke. Unburned plastics matt into an awful polluting mass. Make sure they are burned completely one at a time.

Modern nylon tents are very susceptible to being ruined by flying sparks—keep fires well away, 20 feet away, from tents, sleeping bags and packframes.

utane gas in small canisters ; handy stuff. (*top*) A ghtweight stove for summer se. (*centre*) A similar stove sing raw gas passed through n evaporator for cold winter iking. But the evergreen tandby of the seasoned ackpacker is unleaded petrol nd a pressure stove. (*bottom*) 'ake care not to use inside sealed tent

How you dress for packing is dictated by the season and altitude. A light well-balanced pack and sun hat for summer's lush fields or windproof coveralls and waterproof leggings for out of season or going high

Which just about brings us to a code of respect for the countryside:

NEVER camp without getting permission.

NEVER make open fires unless you have permission or it is perfectly safe to do so.

BURN all rubbish which will burn and take the rest home with you. Bury only excreta.

NEVER startle cattle or game.

ALWAYS leave gates as you found them—open or shut.

NEVER take crops, fruit or plants, nor cause any damage by your passing over stone hedges, growing hedges, trees or fields.

IF someone bars your passing, don't argue. Give a pleasant good day and retrace your steps. A track marked as right of way on an Ordnance Map might be the subject of a local by-law.

LEAVE nothing behind you which marks your passing, only thanks.

Countryfolk are naturally curious and equally cautious people. Strangers are always a mild threat in sparsely populated country. On the other hand, countryfolk are quite delightful, helpful and amusing people. If you call at a remote farmstead for milk or water, be prepared to waste half an hour in conversation about the world in general. Meet brusqueness with pleasantries, not anger. You are taking something from the countryside by your very passing through it. In return you have to be equally prepared to give something back. At the lowest level this might be a few sentences of conversation. In village pubs, enter into the spirit of the group and be outward-going. You will learn much to your advantage and often make a small profit in gifts of food from the over-planted kitchen gardens of the countryfolk. This will make a welcome change in your diet of AFD foods.

If you play some wind instrument—most of us were taught the recorder at school—get back into practice and whip out a lightweight penny whistle if there is music about. Once people around you realize you have something to contribute you will turn the key to another world. If you play the piano well, tinkle a few notes on the bar piano and then try out a well-known song. If feet start tapping and someone buys you a drink, you are in. If there is a stony silence, quietly close the piano lid again.

A good, clean, joke is also another useful gambit in a country pub. But it must be clean, not too sophisticated and not too long winded.

What is more, any joke must be a good one and free from religious undertones. Jokes are like currency, they keep changing hands until everyone has heard them. Then the community gets short of change. A new joke from you will live on in the village long after you have passed. The best jokes are those told against oneself.

In village shops you will be appalled by the slowness of service and the haphazardness of it all. Don't pull your towny attitudes out in the country. Move with the sluggish tide of country life rather than against it. The village store is the bush telegraph station; anything you do which offends will be passed on ahead of you very quickly. Years ago I was on the Knapdale Forest isthmus from the Crinan canal down near the hamlet of Keillmore. A couple of days later I was in a butcher's shop at Lochgilphead 15 miles away and was astonished to hear the butcher say, "Ye must be the camper over at Wullie Boyd's place?" I was. I am no longer astonished at the bush telegraph of the country. A proper conduct in the country can find you a dry barn on a wild night. Disrespect can bring you—and the rest of us—a lot of trouble.

Finding your way around the country can be done in two ways. You can either bomb along, head down and nose twitching on the scent of the wind, or you can use a map. I use a map not only to find my way but also to enrich my time out of doors and give me a lifetime of pleasure by 'reading over' the places I travelled through. If maps make no sense to you, and never will, just keep bombing along and trusting in the Lord.

On the other hand, if maps do mean something to you, become proficient in the use of them and work up a good relationship with your compass, not only to find the position of sun-up, but also finding your way should conditions ever get really bad.

I don't intend to teach you how to use maps and the compass—there are plenty of good reference books which will treat this subject exhaustively. I will only give you a few headings of points at which you should strive for proficiency and leave the map and compass stuff to you:

1. Get the National Grid system under your belt once and for all. Remember read *easterly* (read along the top or bottom of the sheet) first then *northerly*. Be able to use four and six digit references without even thinking about them.

2. Study the key diagram and know all the conventional symbols so that observable features in the near distance can be located on the map with accuracy.
3. Know your contours so that relief stands up in the mind's eye to give you the feel of the country you find yourself in.
4. Get the hang of orienting the map grid to compass north.
5. Using compass and map be able to take an accurate magnetic bearing and transfer it to the open map.
6. By opisometer or by estimation, learn how to lay off distances from a map so that approximate times of arrival at the next halt can be worked out.
7. Always know where you are in case conditions suddenly make further observations impossible.

Any mark on a map should be made with a soft 2B pencil which can be erased. A small cross for a halt with the time pencilled alongside will keep tabs on your progress in difficult country.

Some people keep logs. If you like making notes and can write shorthand, take along a small spiral-bound notebook and a couple of pencils. If you are beach walking, learn about tidal constants and the range of tides. Spring tides, which occur for a few days twice monthly, are *high* tides. Neaps are not so high. There are two high tides every 24 hours and 50 minutes. Discover when these high tides will occur along the route you will be using and note them in the memo book. Due to a lot of factors, high tide does not occur at the same time all along the coast you will be passing so make a note of the *constants* which must be added or subtracted from the high tide times. NEVER walk along flat sand pits, saltings, and beaches hemmed in by rock walls when the tide is flooding. Half an hour after high tide will give you about five hours of travel over ground which is continually uncovering before the tide changes. If you should get trapped on saltings or quicksands, inflate your air mattress or empty the collapsible plastic water bottle for buoyancy. Put empty polybottles in your pockets—even blown up polybags tightly knotted will help. Dump your pack if things look bad and don't panic. Floundering will only make things worse. Attract attention with your whistle. Set fire to your pack if all else fails!

There is another use for your little notebook. A running list of expenses will help you plan your next trip more accurately. And if you buy a few stamps for any messages to civilization you can keep these in safety inside the hard covers of the memo book.

Above all, backpacking demands a special attitude towards the weather—whatever it turns out to be. Everyone loves the sunshine and a pleasant breeze. But many get bad-tempered when it rains or the wind blows keen. Take it all in your stride and modify your programme accordingly. No good sailor works against wind and tide—neither should a lightweighter. If things are setting in badly, stop, make camp and get comfortable before the patch of bad weather turns on the tap. I have given a lot of space to weather watching in chapter five and it will repay you handsomely if you learn to read the signs in the sky accurately.

As I said earlier, no site is ideal when it comes to making camp. But if you continually make a mental note of good places as you pass along and the weather begins to deteriorate it might be a good idea to backtrack a little way to the last spot which looked usable rather than press on in the blind hope that somewhere will open up for you before it chucks it down.

Finally, a few thoughts about hostelling and hitch-hiking.

Youth hostels are a proven way of travelling light. They offer good shelter and a bed for a modest price. For the young who have worrying parents, youth hostelling might be the only way they will find freedom. For students with shallow pockets, youth hostels are often the only way they can travel extensively both at home and abroad.

But youth hostels belong to an institution and the rules, although pared to a minimum, have to be fully obeyed. Hostels are closed during the day. Get stacked out. There are chores to be done. The dormitories are filled up at night with people of different habits and ideas about privacy and silence. A YHA standard sleeping bag is mandatory and must even be worn over your own down sleeping bag if you insist on using it. You can hire bags each night. Hostel life is rather spartan and according to the personality of the warden can be disconcerting to the timid.

Personally, I believe that the low annual membership cost is worth the expenditure if only as an insurance policy for when the weather turns bad. Hostels are safe ramparts in a bad weather landscape, shops for basic commodities and a place to dry out. A good hostel shower every three or four days brings refreshment on the trail. A warden's knowledge of the local terrain is invaluable.

I have not been hitch-hiking for some time, but my son is an inveterate hitch-hiker. I am usually the bloke who picks up hitch-hikers so I will pass along a few tips to people who expect folk like me to stop for them.

Remember the decision of the driver to stop or pass by must be made in a split second. Only a fleeting glance of the person behind the thumb is possible. And it is on this fleeting glance that judgment is formed.

If you intend to hitch don't look dejected, dirty, unkempt and lazy. Lying in the grass with a waving thumb and a town name scrawled on a tatty bit of paper will never do. A driver must see, in that fleeting moment, who is wanting his patronage, and the size of the pack.

Always stand where a driver has room to drop out of the traffic flow without danger to the following vehicles. Look eager. Look right into the driver's eyes and smile. If you don't get a flash of indicators and stop lights from a passing vehicle, don't be tempted to give the old two finger Harvey Smith salute. This can be seen in a rear-view mirror and will quickly make up a mind which was in two thoughts about stopping.

No driver will stop when there is a great posse of hitchers hanging around—he might get lumbered with more than he cares to take along. Drivers stop for many different reasons, but I suspect more than anything else, a driver stops to give a lift to someone who will help him pass the time away on a long journey. Therefore, a hitcher should always open up with a conversation. If the driver is preoccupied with traffic this might fall on apparently deaf ears. Try again later. There is nothing I find more infuriating about a hitcher who jumps into my vehicle, smokes my cigarettes and has nothing to say except where he wants to be set down. Never make yourself at home in someone's car until you are bidden to do so. Leave windows alone until permission to adjust them is given. If safety belts are fitted to the car, belt up—it could save your life.

My son's way with drivers who are drunk, queer, or just downright bad is to keep an eye open for the first hitcher he sees and then firmly asks to be set down because he has 'just seen a friend'. He always notes exactly where the ignition key is located for the final escape route—a switch off and removal of the key—not that he has ever reached this drastic last exit.

I mentioned packs earlier, but it will not go amiss to reiterate that if your mode of travel is going to be entirely hitching, keep your pack small and free of awkward corners which are liable to damage the vehicle in which you are travelling.

Hitching is full of luck. Some days you will get a dozen lifts and only cover as many miles. Other days you will get to John o' Groat's in one lift. Sometimes you will get nowhere. Be flexible—if a good lift is going to an area which you had not considered, take it and work out in your mind what to do during the first few miles.

Writing down names on pieces of paper is considered to be bad form. It also restricts the number of lifts you will be offered. A man going only a dozen miles down the road will likely leave you by, whereas his lift could land you in an area where fat lifts are going begging. If you must hitch after dark, stand just beyond a street light where a driver can see your face, and never walk along the roadside in the dark without wearing retroflective material which will show up in headlights many yards ahead. You could get killed—but easily.

The best map a hitch-hiker can use in Britain is the Ordnance Survey Route Planning Map. Abroad buy a petrol company map.

Always treat a driver's car with respect—after all, it represents a considerable investment to him, and wetting his upholstery through or trampling mud into his carpet is not the best way of repaying him for his kindness.

Finally, something I saw a long time ago might give encouragement to those who are weak of heart or wind, or those with afflictions of the spine and shoulders which prevent them wearing a pack, but who would dearly love to go travelling light.

Don't scorn the perambulator or a custom-made rig built on the same lines. This fellow I saw had lost an arm and there was something wrong with his rib cage too. But he had persuaded someone to build him a four-wheeled vehicle rather like a pram on which was an aluminium superstructure which contained a kitchen and storage hold for all his lightweight gear. It worked like a charm as he pushed his way along the minor roads of Derbyshire on a tour which had began by rail and was finished by rail. He travelled alone and was a shining example of someone really doing his own thing. It makes you think.

5

Keeping a weather eye open

There is a fragment of old school physics which begins, "The atmosphere is a fluid in constant motion. . . ." It is this fluid bit which bothers every backpacker who lives out of doors for more than a couple of days together. And so if there is one thing he should do, besides protecting himself from the fluids, it is learn more about what is going on up there and takes steps accordingly. There will always be the question: to press on or to lay up? running through the mind of anyone who goes out of doors for fun. Closeness to that fluid in constant motion can turn a weekend of pleasure into a miserable experience for anyone not prepared to either listen to weather forecasts broadcast by the professionals or take steps to learn the rudiments of weather forecasting for himself.

The modern lightweight radio set, providing it has long wave and medium wave reception, is the easiest way of being forewarned. London Weather Centre goes to considerable trouble to keep everyone within radio earshot well informed. But what if you don't want to carry that extra weight, or the batteries give out, what then?

Fortunately, the fluid in constant motion also gives those with sufficient skill in observation ample warning signs to be read before the fluid becomes manifest. I have already told you about my early morning habit--no, not that one—of peeping out from under the flysheet and making a decision about immediate plans. It is a knack I have inherited from my father who could sniff the air, con the sky and declare that the family should go out of doors when everyone else had given up the day for lost. Usually he was irritatingly right, and I just had to learn this magic for myself. You too can become a weather magician if you are willing to keep your eyes open and make records and notes. Practised over a lifetime, single station weather forecasting is great fun.

Obviously, in the short space of this chapter, I can only begin to turn you into an instant weather forecaster. But with a short excursion into the physical world and some explanation I might just interest you enough to want to go on.

Now if we lightweighters could be astronauts for a moment and some secret invention could turn the world's atmosphere into a seeable opaque mass for a little while we should see heaves and hollows wherever we looked down, as though the atmosphere had turned into driven snow or drifting sand. You can get some idea of this effect if you look at every Saturday's weather page in the *Guardian*. This newspaper has had the inspiration to print a picture captured on Friday afternoons when an orbiting United States weather satellite is over the British Isles. Because cloud formations follow very definite patterns of the atmosphere in action, and the scale of the picture seen from on high gives only large detail, you can begin to 'feel' this heaving and depressing of the atmosphere.

Unfortunately, the lightweighter trundling along his lonely way can only see the heavens from underneath and over a very small compass. Even so, there is usually enough advance warning in the local sky patterns to give time for avoiding action.

Take a squint at figure 7. This diagram depicts the British Isles divided into four quarters. Those winds blowing in from the north-easterly quarter are called by weathermen continental polar (cP) and bring sharply cold conditions and often accompanied by low sheet clouds and clammy cold mists on the east coast and eastern ranges of hills. They originated in Siberia and northern Scandinavia, so we expect the cold they bring, and because the North Sea is not a very big ocean they have not become heavy with rain.

Winds blowing in from the south-easterly quarter are called continental tropical (cT) and originate as far south as the Sahara Desert. They bring warm, or very warm air over a dry continent and are often cloudless with a slight haze. Unfortunately there are not enough days in the year when the cT air masses head for Britain.

The south-westerly quarter is the origin of most of the air streams coming to our islands. Called maritime tropical (mT) they have had a long ride over the ocean sucking up much moisture into their warm hearts and the first land mass in the way gets the lot chucked on it. Any mT stuff can be guaranteed to be cloudy, rainy and drizzly with poor visibility.

The north-westerly quarter is dominated by two types of air masses, maritime polar (mP) and returning maritime polar (rmP). This latter stuff has probably been here before as mT, passed around a depression to the north, and come back for a second attack. Fortunately most of the fluid stuff has been dropped and rmP air is relatively dry and cool with good visibility. The ground observer without a peep at weather charts would not be able to distinguish rmP from maritime polar (mP). North-westerly winds laden with a

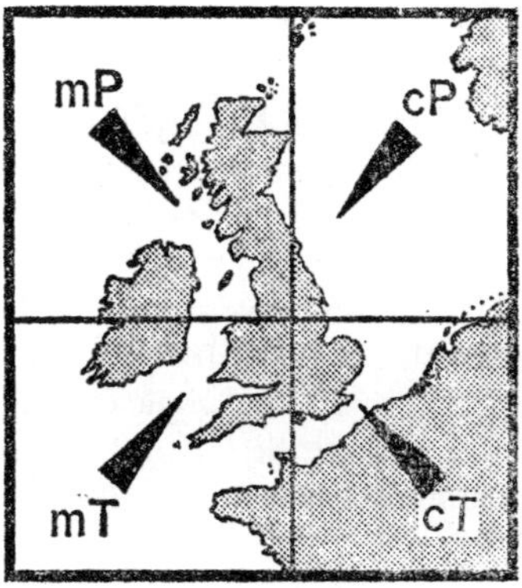

Figure 7

few cold showers also give way between the showers to very bright, cool periods and good visibility.

Would that weather forecasting were as simple as this. Although we now understand the type of weather coming from a particular direction, we must also understand a few other phenomena.

'Fronts' are something the weathermen refer to quite often. Let me try to explain, and then we can go on to see what happens when they are lurking about.

For simplicity let us call all the air surrounding the poles cold air, and air around the equator warm air. Somewhere the two air masses will meet and rub against each other. Mixing is quite poor and there is a lot of energy released as the massive cold and warm forces do a face-to-face. As the rubbing action develops the interface folds and waves. Downcoming cold air pushing southwards is called a 'cold front' and the corresponding upwards push of warm air is called a 'warm front'.

As the rubbing action increases eddies begin to form—rather like the eddies at the confluence of two streams. These eddies are depressions or 'lows'. Because in the northern hemisphere they rotate clockwise they are said to be 'cyclonic'.

'Anticyclones' are heaps of heavier air called 'highs'. Winds blow outwards from the perimeters of highs towards the lows trying to fill them up. Winds blow inwards towards the centres of lows trying to fill them up until all the energy is lost and the weather system peters out and becomes stable again before the next system rolls in behind.

We in the middle latitudes have to put up with all the air mixing and its associated lows, highs and fronts. According to the time of year, weather systems will swing across the British Isles in hours or days. Only in summer when the traditional anticyclone develops over the Azores, and sends the fronts packing over the northern part of Scotland, do we get settled weather for days on end. In autumn we often experience a large anticyclone right over Europe and stationary for days. This high also blocks off the normal weather pattern and gives us those balmy Indian Summer patches at the end of September and in October.

This brief description of the main phenomena is necessary to understand the nature of fronts as they affect the lonely lightweighter trying to decide whether to make camp or press on for a while longer.

Figure 8 shows a chart of a typical depression and its associated fronts. The lines are called isobars and indicate a contour of all the places on the ground having the same barometric pressure. As the depression approaches the pressure slowly subsides and the first feathery wisps of cirrus (Ci) riding on the jet-stream high overhead will be fanning their way eastwards. At a much lower level, there will be puffy cotton wool clouds of fair weather cumulus (Cu) with the characteristic flat bottoms. Now, if the lightweighter will stop for a moment and lie on his back, he will observe much. First of all he must watch the high cirrus and the direction it is taking. Now he must check the lower cumulus and note its direction. If the lower clouds are crossing the path of the higher clouds from the *right* then there is a depression on its way. This is position A in figure 8. This depression means a worsening of the weather with frontal rain to follow.

Figure 9 shows a diagram of a cross section through a warm front, and the high mare's tails of cirrus are a common early warning sign of an approaching warm front. As the front develops there will be a thin sheet of featureless cirrostratus (Cs) form, probably in association with patches of mackerel sky or cirrocumulus (Cc). Look for a halo around the sun or the moon to spot the cirrostratus. A scan from horizon to horizon will also reveal that the fair weather cumulus clouds have disappeared—cut off from the strong heat of the sun by the high clouds the cumulus can no longer get up steam.

Once you have observed these things, make camp, because you have only two or three hours—perhaps less—in which to prepare for the rain. As the wedge of warm air climbs over the back of the coolish air in which you will be standing, so heavier and heavier cloud will form. At first it is fairly high up and a mixture of ice and rain rises and falls inside the cloud with only a small amount reaching the ground. Later the heavy mob of nimbo-stratus (Ns) clouds bring up the waterworks and down she comes. By now the observant lightweighter should be fed, pitched and ready to hole up. Most warm fronts seem to me to approach Britain during the afternoon and fortunately this gives time for an early night halt and an excuse to grab some extra sleep.

Gradually the warm front lumbers past. But behind every warm front—position B in figure 8—there is a cold front trying to catch up. If you are well south of the depression there will be a period of partial clearing of the skies. Bright periods and showers in the muggy air. This is the warm sector and the air will definitely feel warmer to you. But a close look over the horizon on the south-westerly quarter should soon reveal bands of big puffy clouds with grey faces and all strung out in a long line. This, chaps, is the expected cold front. Get under cover and stay there, you are now approaching position C in figure 8.

Cold fronts don't mess about the way that warm fronts do. The deluge is quick and heavy. The wind picks up and fills in from the north-westerly quarter and hammers at wet canvas, so whenever you are waiting for a cold front to arrive, fill in the time with an inspection of guys and pegs.

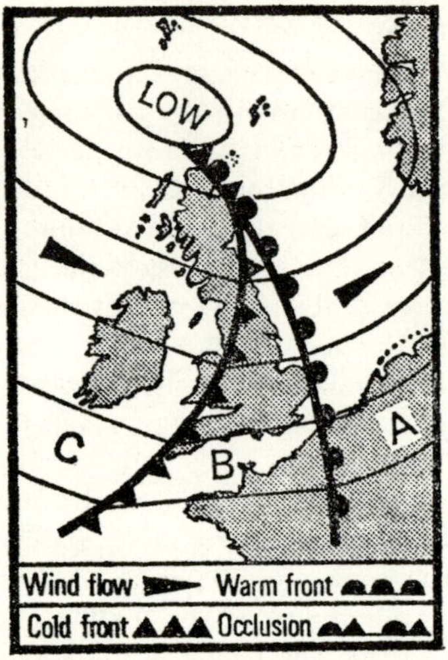

Figure 8

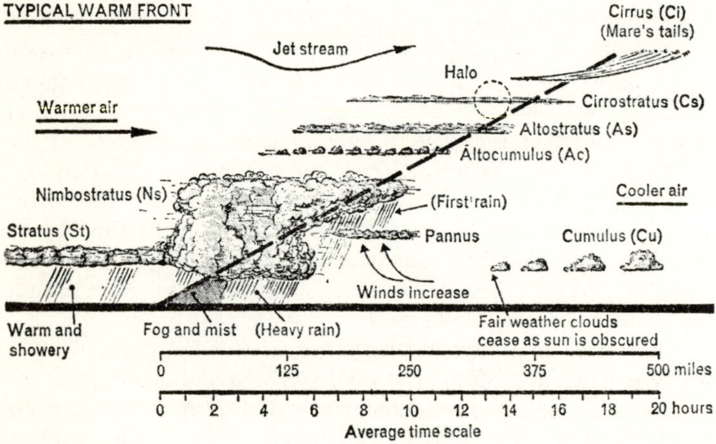

Figure 9

In the wake of the cold front there is clear, well-washed greeny-blue skies filled with lurching grey monsters looking like enormous cauliflowers. Underneath each towering cumulonimbus (Cb) is the characteristic black diagonal hatching of a heavy rain storm. Sometimes these noisy monsters have anvil-shaped heads of false cirrus trailing out before them. The bigger the cloud the bigger the damage they can do. Rain, hail, thunder and vicious winds pack these clouds with a terrible punch. If you see one approaching and you are in open country find shelter as soon as possible.

By now the depression will be well away to the east. The path of the few high clouds visible will be crossed by the lower cloud from the *left* and eventually all the clouds will be going in roughly the same direction down wind. Load up and get a move on before the next lot of mare's tails slaver over the western horizon.

What I have described is a model warm front and cold front passage associated with a depression to the north of the observer. In practice there will be several modifying factors but the main features will remain. As the observer becomes proficient so he is able to spot confused weather patterns and read the early warning signs accordingly.

Tapping a barometer looks impressive and to the trained observer

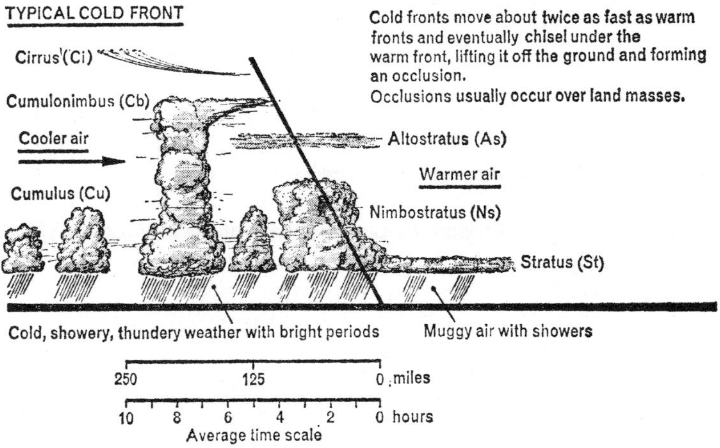

Figure 10

it does have its place. Even a badly adjusted barometer, often found in the country pub, will give the tapper an indication of the trend—don't let the landlord see you tapping his barometer though, some folk get quite shirty about this. A slow fall indicates a depression on its way; a rapid fall, a barrel full of wind followed by squally rain. A big upwards jump indicates a cold front passing through. A steady barometer, no change.

There are other signs for the experienced eye. Swallows and swifts which feed off insects on the wind follow their quarry to the height at which the insects are supported by the density of the air. High flying swifts, swallows and martins, indicate an anticyclone or high pressure region. The winds will be from the north-easterly quarter, coolish and perhaps some sheet cloud. Little change.

Midges and gnats swarming in the evening air by the hedgerow after rain indicate that the warm front has passed and there is now a warm sector drifting through. Look for shafts of evening sunshine from under layers of cloud and prepare for the cold front which is just over the horizon and likely to hammer through in the night or early morning.

A brassy sun-up rarely lasts bright the whole day through, and to wake up to grass without dew is a suspicious sign. Dew forms when the clear night skies draw off heat radiated from the ground. If high clouds of an approaching warm front have cut off the radiation, dew is prevented from forming. Con the western horizon for Cs or Cc and get breakfast over before the first raindrops fall.

The best mornings are aften misty with a heavy dew. The sun is a golden wash of light to the east and the orb hard to define. The tent will be saturated with moisture and your footsteps clearly marked in the soaked grass. Such a morning should bring a glorious hot day which will last through to suppertime.

Clear horizons and pin-sharp detail of objects a long way off tends to mean an increase in winds up to fresh or gale force—generally from the south-east or southerly quarter.

Aircraft flying high overhead leaving contrails give a clue to the condition of the upper air where the jetstreams run. If the cross wind conditions I described earlier are forming when the lower clouds cross the path of the spreading contrail from the right, be warned. If contrails disappear quickly after the aircraft has passed, this usually indicates settled weather.

Clear evening skies after a hot day will cause the thermometer to tumble fast in the hours after midnight. Unless your camp is on higher ground than the valley below you will be in for a chilly night.

The little weather maps I have drawn in figure 11 are typical charts you will see on your television screens or in your newspapers. To help you plan for the coming weekend, try and match the actual chart with one of my typical patterns and lay your plans accordingly. If you enjoy making weather charts, you can reproduce the shipping forecast chart in figure 12 and by pasting this map between two thin sheets of plastic, follow the shipping forecast on 1,500 metres as the announcer works his way around.

Before the area forecasts the announcer will give a brief synopsis. "Low, 998, South-east Iceland. High 1026 northern France. A trough across Faeroes, Hebrides, Malin to Shannon."

This gives the main picture. Then he will carry on with the area forecast. "Viking, Forties. South-westerly, four. Good . . ." This gives a plot of the wind direction and strength and some indication of the expected weather.

Finally comes a résumé of past weather from the eleven coastal stations beginning at Wick and ending at Tiree. The Shannon report is always of significance because it is usually upwind of us in England and Wales and will give some indication of expected weather in the next two or three hours.

Draw your weather chart on the plastic sheet with a wax crayon and rub it out for the next forecast. If you cannot be bothered with single station observing, take a small radio along and put your faith in the man at the London Weather Centre. He is likely to be right on 65 per cent of his forecasts.

One point I should bring to the attention of mountain walkers. Because much of our weather is mT—wet stuff coming from the south-west—it follows that any land from south Devon round to the Mull of Kintyre and the Isle of Skye will take the brunt of what is coming over the south-westerly horizon. As this moist air rises rapidly over a mountain range of coastal hillside it will lose its ability to hold its water. This accounts for westerly hilltops being wreathed in cloud when the coast at sea level is enjoying bright patches or sunlight between the puffy clouds. If you want to go into the mountains, and you are not a trained mountain man, keep a morning eye open for the first cloud forming in top of the range.

A. Warm front approaching. Rainy weekend imminent, with strong to gale-force southerly to south-westerly winds at first. Unsettled generally.

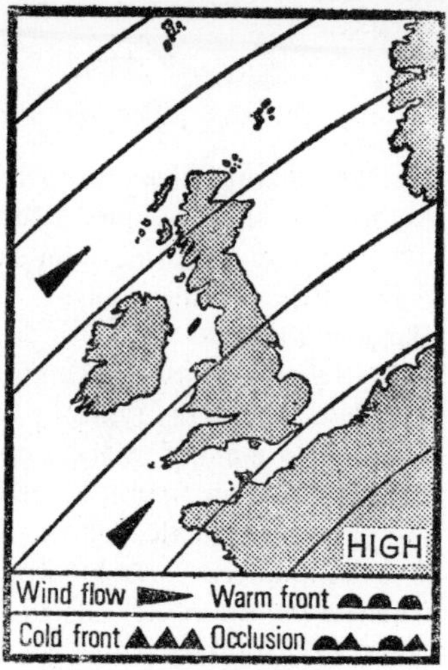

B. Indian summer weather. A big anticyclone over Europe gives unexpected warm weather and holds off Atlantic weather patterns. Grab the weekend as a bonus.

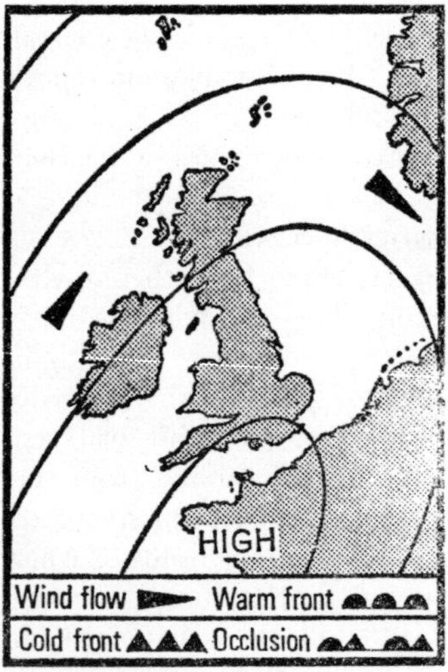

C. Azores ridge dominates British weather. Manly fair everywhere with cool winds on eastern coast and some local rain in hills to the west. Thunder could develop in the south-east in August.

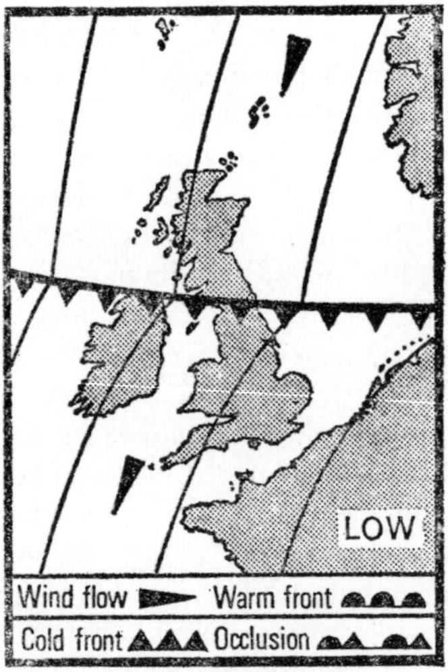

D. Cold front is sliding down the British Isles. Typical March-April weather pattern with mainly clear skies. Cold northerly winds and a few sharp showers. Beware of exposure risks in high places despite the sunshine.

Figure 11. Friday weather patterns

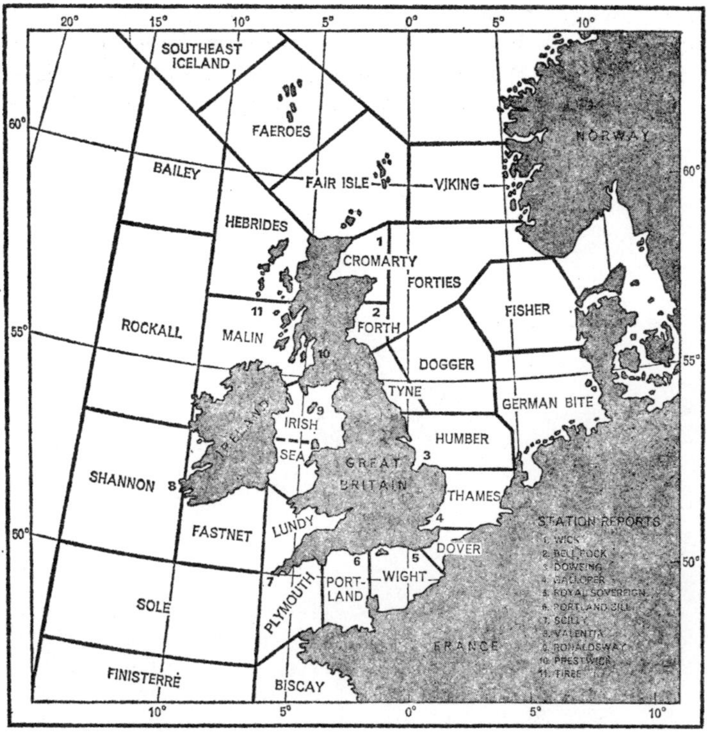

Figure 12. Shipping weather forecast areas. Forecasts are broadcast daily at 0630, 1355, 1755 and 0030 hours on 1,500m (200kHz). Broadcast begins with a general synopsis followed by area by area forecasts beginning with Viking and ending with South-east Iceland. A report of past weather from coastal station completes the broadcast. The BBC transmits other weather forecasts for land areas on medium wavelengths at regular intervals. For timing consult the *Radio Times*.

This is a sure indication of bad conditions to come in the mountains behind. Better to stay on the coast than get wet or lost. Orographic rain is quite as bad as any frontal rain and because it is local it will not usually be mentioned by the man at the London Weather Centre, so beware.

If I have excited your interest in weather and its forecasting I am very pleased. I would suggest a fine little cloud atlas and weather forecasting book by Alan Watts and published by Adlard Coles. Although *Instant Weather Forecasting* is only a slim little volume it is a worthwhile addition to any backpacker's bookshelf.

6

Doing your own thing

When we launched out on this book together, I writing and you reading, I quite overlooked the fact that you might not be able to afford all the things which have come to me over the years. I also ignored that urge in many people to make as much as is possible at home and own the minimum of shop-bought things which only an expert can build. So for all the do-it-your-selfers, I now make some amends in this chapter by examining articles of kit which can be made at home or on the trail.

Let's begin by exploring ways with polythene sheeting. This wonder material of the plastics age is blown in tubular form from a machine which heats up a powder. As it rises in the machine the tube passes over rollers to retain the blowing pressure. This final tubular form has many advantages which the amateur cannot reproduce, for joining or sealing polythene sheeting is beyond the stick of most adhesives and types of heat sealing which can be done with a soldering iron or flat iron at home.

For instance, a length of 350 mil tube which when folded flat measures four feet across, can be turned into a tube tent in minutes. Buy about nine feet of the stuff and 30 feet of 500-pound test plaited nylon cord and you are in business. Halve the nylon cord and heat seal the ends. Then rob another good foot off each piece, heat sealing the ends again. Halve the short pieces and heat seal up once more.

Before venturing forth into the wilderness, rig the tube tent in the back garden this way. Firstly, find six smooth pebbles about an inch in diameter in the flower bed. Take the long lengths of nylon cord and push one of the pebbles into the natural crease of the polythene from the inside about three inches in. Gather up the blob of pebble and polythene so formed in a clove hitch (see figure 14) and pull it tight. Run along the same natural crease to the far end and push another pebble in and repeat the knot with the other long length of cord. Make a mark with a felt pen about two-thirds the way across the tube from one natural crease towards the other—on both ends and sides. Stuff the remaining pebbles in at these points from the inside as with the long lengths of cord and you should be left with four pigtails—two at each end.

Fashion up four tent pegs from any bit of stick and set up your polybivvy this way. Tie the end of one long guy to the garden fence about five feet from the ground and run across to the other fence hauling up the sheet fairly taut. Secure temporarily.

Now peg out the bottom of the tube until the floor is quite taut and flat and then resecure the temporary guyline to the garden fence, cherry tree or whatever. Inside this triangular-shaped tube you can be quite snug in summer weather even in a rainstorm if you have been lucky enough to find two trees or garden fences which will allow you to rig the shelter at right angles to the incoming rain-wind.

If you are in open country and have to bivvy out of the rain, try tying one end of the tube together as though you were tying up a sack and attach a short length of cord to this end. Peg down. Using your packframe as an upright at the other end, haul down on the long guy and peg securely. Now peg out the bottom as before. Inside this tapering tube your kit will remain fairly dry and you should find a good night's sleep. There will be condensation but if you can find some springy green ash sapling to make a hoop to push down near the foot end of the tube the moisture will stay mostly where it is and not soak into your sleeping bag.

Polythene tube of this size and weight will cost only pence and give you adequate summer shelter for several nights away from home. Your shelter will weigh only about 1 pound 3 ounces if you throw the pebbles away each morning and find new ones each night.

This pebble and line method of securing polythene is the best way I know of converting cheap plastics material into useful tentage.

Make a cooking shelter to your standard tent. Set up your tent in the normal way, tail to the wind. Now cut a piece of polytube down one side and open it out. Drape it over the entrance to your tent in such a way as to give the most space with the best use of your existing guy lines and ones you can attach to the polythene by the pebble and clove hitch method. With some ingenuity it is surprising how much extra space can be built to a tent for a penalty of only a few ounces of polythene.

I generally prefer to have a kitchen some way from the tent and I try to employ stone walls, depressions in the ground, trees and shrubs to give me the best stand for the attachment of my polythene sheeting. The sheeting forms the windproof side and a lean-to roof gives ample protection from the elements for cooking and eating at overnight stops. On beaches, polythene comes into its own when wrapped around a wigwam of driftwood set hard into the sand on one end and all gathered up with a bit of cord at the top. The chinks between the sticks of driftwood are made windproof by draping polythene sheeting around the outside. Inside will be snug and the fire will throw heat into the wigwam to warm the tired body while supper is cooked.

If you are in open country where water is hard to get, set up a big piece of polythene as a reservoir to catch rain water. Rain water usually makes horrible morning tea but is fine for washing out socks and sunburned faces. The easiest form of reservoir is made by setting a sheet stretched out along an exposed wall and then tapering the other end and guying it downwards so that rain will trickle into the largest billy you have. Secure it well or the wind will take charge of it.

There's not much room in a small hike tent so I generally make a polythene-covered bundle of all the things which have no business in the tent during the night. If the bundle is secured well and anchored with big stones all your kit will be quite dry in the morning.

A 6-foot length of 4-foot wide polytube of 350 gauge will make a reasonable poncho if you cannot afford a good cagoule in your first season of going light. Cut one end so that one side is high and the other dips. Slip the whole tube over the body from the feet first—never the other way round—and drag the longer edge right over your head to make a shawl with it. The shorter edge will come up under the chin, and an elastic band will secure the rig tolerably well. Alternatively, you can cut a circle about ten feet in diameter from an opened tube of 5-foot polythene. In the middle cut a hole just large enough for your neck and a slit to allow your head to pass through. After donning your towel like a scarf pop the poncho right over your head. A sou'wester goes on top.

A sheet of polythene under your tent prevents mud and worm casts soiling the nylon.

This by no means exhausts all the things you can do with polythene and its slightly heavier, but more robust cousin, vinyl. These two plastic sheetings are science's gift to the lightweighter and I am grateful. Just make sure you burn it up when you have no further use for a piece. Nothing is quite as bad as plastics for littering up the countryside.

The YHA Services among other places sells urethane-coated nylon cloth in various weights, widths and colours. If you are handy with a sewing machine you might like to make up your own tent, overtrousers or leggings and cagoule at home. But let me warn you that cutting out and running up lightweight nylons is no easy matter for the amateur. One trick I have learned is simple when you consider it. Buy a tin of Cow Gum—you will find it in artists' material shops and drawing office suppliers—and thinly coat the nylon where the seams are to be made. When the rubber gum has dried the parts can be brought together and the seam neatly formed before the sewing takes place. Since most seams have to be doped to make them waterproof this gumming with a rubber solution helps the finished product in two ways. Use only good linen thread with nylon waterproof garments and tents. The thread swells with rain and helps to close the oversize hole made by the sewing machine needle.

Start your sewing circle with an unambitious pair of rain chaps or leggings. They are simple to cut out and sew up and save a good deal of money. Leggings take quite a bashing in the scrub and heather so you can afford a new pair of home-made ones every time they leak. Cagoules are much harder to make. Borrow one as a pattern and try your hand. But don't try too much fancy tailoring to begin with. The looser the fit the better it should be.

The all-purpose tarp to replace polythene as a shelter is well within the amateur sewer's repertoire, but anything less than ten feet by eight is hardly worth making. Use nylon tapes for suspension points and sew them on everywhere you might think they will be useful, because sure as eggs you will not have enough tie points on your tarp when you come to rig it.

True tents are ambitious projects only for the gifted. If you must make a tent in urethane-proofed nylon, try something simple and then you will not be disappointed, nor will you have wasted quite a lot of good expensive nylon cloth.

One good saving the handy sewer can make is the packsack to fit on a factory-made packframe. But be warned, much of the stitching will be hand work and getting zip fasteners just right is difficult.

Sleeping bags and duvet clothing are beyond all but the most skilled of home builders. If you don't want the house layered in down for months to come, leave this costly but essential equipment to the specialists.

If you are handy with metal, try making a pot iron for the fire from a piece of stainless steel rod about ⅛-inch in diameter. A simple three point job about ten inches across and splayed open to about four inches on one side will be just about right. The apex of the triangle and the two ends can be turned down about half an inch to give perfect three point suspension.

The steel bail of the frypan of the Bulldog Hobo outfit can be lightened by drilling holes across it

Most tent poles can be replaced with lighter gauge, thinner walled alloy tubing. This is a job any amateur can tackle. Look around the metal parts of your kit and see if they can be redesigned, replaced in aluminium or done away with. Every ounce saved. . . .

From time to time you will have accidents with your kit while you are out on a trip. Nylons and plastics are easily destroyed by heat and holed by sparks from a camp fire. Even ripstop nylon will rip on thorns and barbed wire fences.

Field repairs are not made easily with needle and thread. And who wants to be sewing when there is sunshine to be enjoyed? What suits me might suit you. Remember my aluminium canister which holds my windproof flamers and striker—it once contained 'Anadin' tablets? Well, around this former I have a length of 1-inch wide electrician's vinyl impact-adhesive tape. Several lengths, in fact, wound side by side. This wonderful stuff sticks well to nylon fabrics found in tents, duvet clothing and sleeping bags. A good patch on a damaged area will keep out the rain or keep in the precious down until I can get home and make a proper repair with a fine needle. The same tape will make a sound repair to the pneumatic frame used in the BB 'Ariel' rucksack too.

As well as adhesive tape I can recommend good-quality rubberbands for the odd hold-together job. Keep a few in your first aid kit and they will make good packfriends.

If you have a wife, girl friend or mother who is handy with the knitting pins, you are in luck. Start them off with a simple item of kit, such as a wool hat with ample roll down. This piece of cold-weather equipment is invaluable—it is hard to find a soft woollen balaclava hat these days. Another, and more costly piece of kit is a substitute for the heavy wool mackinaw shirt. To my mind, the shirt found in the outfitter's shop is far from ideal. Much better would be a loose-fitting tightly knitted guernsey with a small collar and instead of buttons down the front a full length of 'Velcro' tape. This tape would give the infinite variety of ventilation to suit the various kinds of going you will find. The collar should have enough upstand to give the proper protection in the neckhole when wearing a cagoule in wet weather.

I once got hold of these heavy guernseys for all the family in unbleached natural oiled wool and they have lasted for years. I don't think you can ever wear the stuff out. The oily texture of the wool is not unpleasant and seems to resist the uptake of moisture from the body and the atmosphere.

Patch pockets over each breast should be made from material rather than wool because they will pull out of shape with stuff shoved in them. Waist pockets would be an added advantage. Plain knitting is preferable to Arran or fancy patterning. Patterning only adds unnecessary weight without increasing the insulating qualities very much.

Heavy woollen mitts are another item of kit which can be made at home to save money. But only the expert can knit boot socks to give the right fit. A poor fit will guarantee blisters.

Trousers can be modified by any deft home dressmaker to give the right sort of garment for walking. Poke around the ex-government stores and look for the crudely cut but high quality clothing made for such people as civil defence and the armed forces. The cloth is usually heavy quality blazer-cloth or melton. Colours are dark and the cut vile. But never mind—for a few pounds you have the makings of a first-class pair of tough trousers—complete with leg patch pockets.

Re-tailor the trousers to leave plenty of seat room but tapering in towards the ankle. The waist-band is miles too high—except if you intend to wear braces, and the seams have too much material in them. But there is nothing that a few hours with the pressing iron, sewing machine and tailor's scissors cannot remedy. And the result: a pair of the hardest-wearing walking trousers that ordinary camp outfitters cannot supply.

A friend of mine spied a pair of dark-blue civil defence trousers in a back-street shop and now he has a fine item of autumn and spring walking gear. I never hear him complain about the wind any more.

Another piece of clothing you can make at home to save a few pence are moccasins. Practically every camp outfitter sells the Canadian kits which contain all the parts cut out to shape and pierced ready for thonging. These kits are fine but if you are ambitious you can see your local cobbler and start from scratch. Leatherwork is very satisfying as a winter hobby and once you have made one pair the whole family is sure to want moccasins too!

While you are doing the odd winter's night job you might modify your Ever Ready 'Minilight' torch. Empty out the batteries. Now scrounge a meat skewer from the kitchen drawer and heat the end over your butane stove while holding the other end in a pair of pliers. Firmly hold the hot skewer against the narrow side of the torch body about half-way down and in a trice the skewer will be through. Remove the heat quickly and allow to cool.

Now cut a lanyard of fine nylon cord long enough to go around your neck and hang to your waist. Heat seal the end of the remaining hank with a match or a quick pass over the butane stove flame. Thread both ends of the cord through the hole you have made in the torch body and pass them up enough to make a large overhand knot. Clip the knotted ends quite short so that no surplus remains and fuse with the flame of a match. Now pop back the batteries and the bulb end of the torch and another job is done. I have said it before, but I make no apology for saying it again. Keep both batteries the same way up until you need to use the torch and then turn one cell over to complete the series circuit. In this way you will get into the habit—a habit which could save your vital batteries against accidental daytime switch-on. It could even save your life.

I think this is about the place to get knotted.

I am constantly amazed that so many people have such a blind spot about tying efficient knots. The right knot for the job in hand is so essential that no lightweight traveller can afford to venture out without learning the basic group.

The most important of all is the bowline. Every time you need a loop which will not slip or close up you need a bowline. Look at the cords tensioning the backbands of your pack and you will see the need for a bowline. If you are lowering your pack over the edge of some difficult rockwork before climbing down yourself you will need a bowline. Bowlines crop up everywhere so here is how they are made.

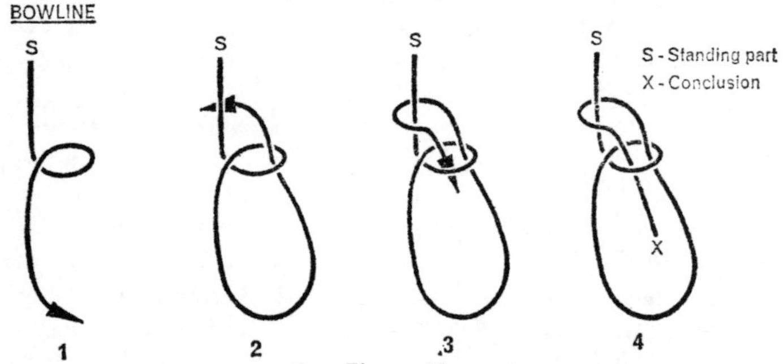

Figure 13

Take the standing part—that is the end which is fixed to somewhere else—in your left hand and with a reasonable amount of the running end make an overhand loop. Pinch this loop with your left thumb and forefinger so that it cannot drop out. Now pass the running part up from behind and through the loop then back over and behind the standing part, right round the back and down into the loop again. Draw the knot tight and it's made. Simple, isn't it? Try it again and again until you are bowline perfect.

The next most commonly used knot is the clove hitch. You will use it on temporary shelters with polythene, attaching cords to round objects such as packframes, trees, poles and the like.

Take the running part and reeve it once around the round object to which you want to make an attachment. As the loop comes around put your left thumb under and continue running around again over the top of the last loop and back through where your thumb is keeping a space waiting. Pull it tight—after you have removed your thumb. That is the clove hitch.

CLOVE HITCH

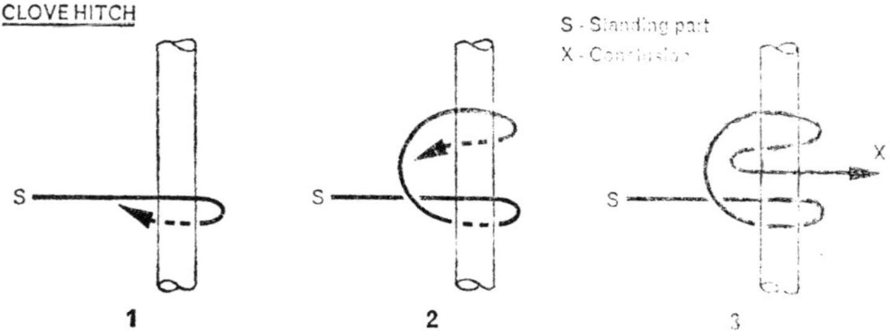

Figure 14

ROUND TURN AND TWO HALF HITCHES

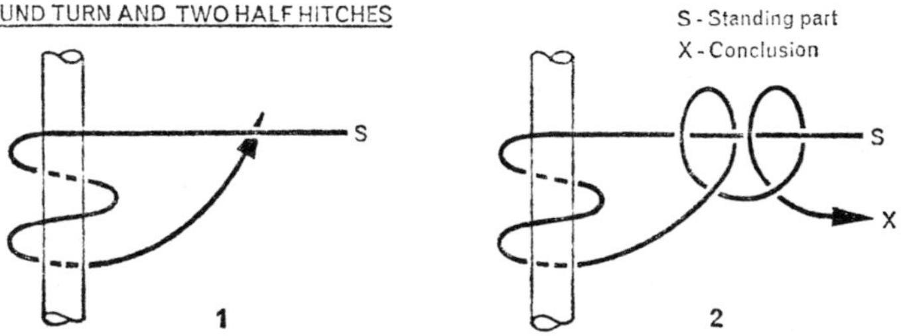

Figure 15

REEF KNOT

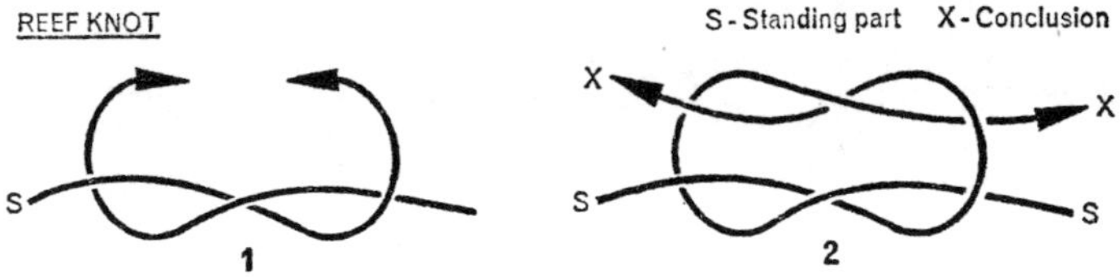

Figure 16

SHEET BEND

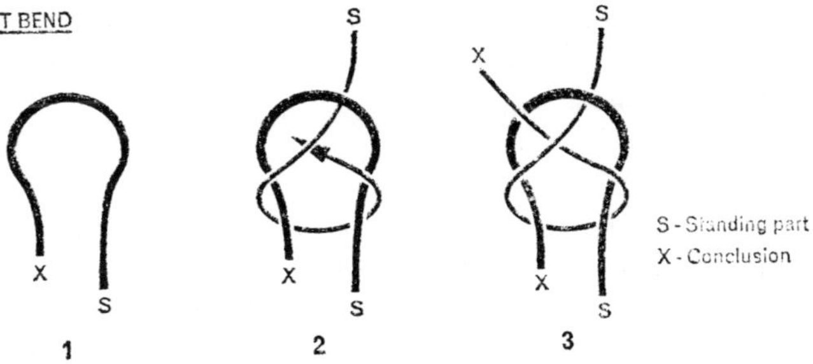

Figure 17

Some people use a round turn and two half-hitches to do a similar thing. Reeve the running end round the object twice and then tie two half-hitches over the standing lines. Only use this knot when you forget how to do a clove hitch.

The reef knot has passed into folk art with its left-over-right right-over-left routine. You can tell when you have made a proper reef knot by the nice shape of friendship it forms. Reef knots are quite good for joining together two ropes or cords of similar size. When one is larger than the other you will use a sheet bend. This simple knot is made with an overhand loop on the end of the thicker piece and passing the thinner end up through this loop and round the back of the standing part before dropping it back down the loop again. It works like a charm if you ease it tight before putting a load on it.

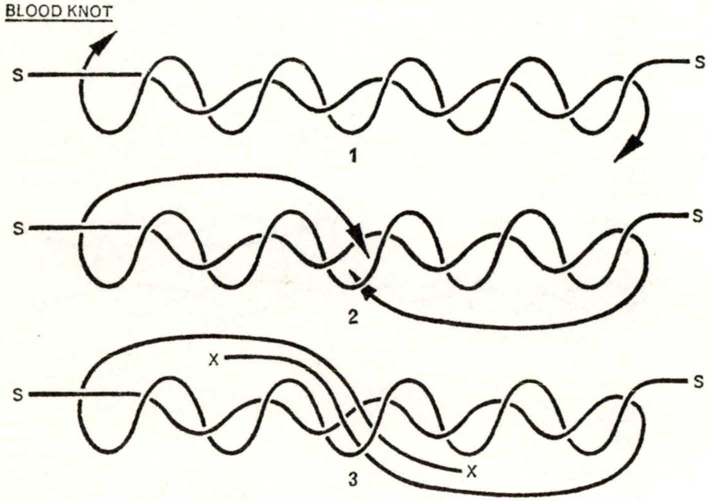

Figure 18

Nylon cord has a nasty habit of slipping so you might like to learn how to join pieces with a fisherman's blood knot. It looks difficult but in practice it is quite simple. A minimum of four twists each side is necessary for a safe job.

Backpackers should also learn how to make a tarbuck knot.

This clever updating of the tautline knot will save an ounce or so on your tent guylines by eliminating the sliders yet provide all the advantages of the metal bits it replaces. A close inspection shows the tarbuck has some origins in the blood knot and that is why it is so efficient in nylon cordage.

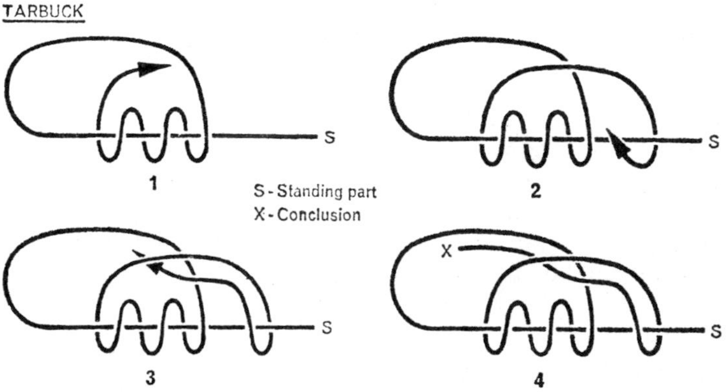

Figure 19

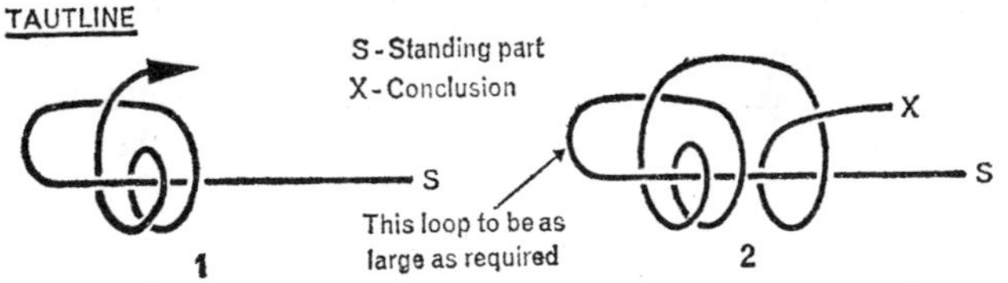

Figure 20

So make big loops to pass round the tent peg and with the running end wrap it around the standing part about four times inwards *towards* the loop. Now bring the end up over the top of the twisted bit you have just made, around the back of the standing part and back down in to the loop so formed. When pulled down tight this knot will resist any slipping of the loop so long as there is a load on it, but the whole knot can be slid up and down the standing side of the loop. You can sleep quite easy in your mind with a tent set up on tarbucks.

Of course, if you wish, you can go on to learn a load of fancy knots to amuse yourself on stormy days when you are bound up inside the tent. Me, I shall just go to sleep in my sleeping bag.

The main point of the exercise is to understand this simple group of essential knots and practise them until they can be done blindfolded or on a stormy, wet and pitch-black night. You never need a proper knot until you need one badly.

Keep your hanks of nylon cordage tidily wrapped up and in an outside pocket of your packsack. Besides making guylines, these various lengths of cordage will provide you with lashings, clotheslines, spare bootlaces, spare trouser belt, handlines for crossing rapidly flowing brooks and small rivers if you *must* do some fording; will tie together temporary shelters from driftwood on beaches, lower gear over difficult rock ledges, lash up rations, spare clothing and a cagoule into a comfortable bundle for making a day hike from a fixed camp, lift water from a well, and heaven knows what else. You could be unlucky and have a failure in some essential part of your pack harness. Only a supply of nylon cordage could get you home in reasonable comfort.

Turning to gadgets, I saw a little gadget my friend—the one with the civil defence trousers—made for himself which impressed me no end when we had our last camp together. It was the end of October and a hunter's moon was in full bloom. There in the moonlight he cooked supper easing over the food with a little home-made aluminium spatula no bigger than a wage packet. The clever thing about it was the handle—a wooden spring-backed clothes peg, one of the two he always carries. When not being used to cook food the pegs secure his washing or dish cloth for drying on the main tent guy.

This same friend is full of novel ha'penny ideas. He collects a special plastic bag used by Post Offices to keep change in known values. These bags seal themselves with a fold-over flap. My friend uses them to keep herbs in—he is a great one with culinary arts.

In a clear plastic pot which used to contain honey he keeps a thick stearin candle. The candle burns brightly without much flittering and amazes me by not melting the plastic pot. Set up in the end of the tent on a canteen it seems safe enough. Another thing this resourceful man does is to tape two 2p pieces to the back of his home-made map case, "for the phone, you know". This map case was made from two sheets of clear plastic taped down three sides.

The case is big enough to take a one-inch sheet without its covers. He always buys the flat sheets and folds them himself.

My friend envies my little gadget, a tiny, but accurate thermometer. I salvaged it from one of my son's Christmas presents of a few years back. Made in Hong Kong and supposed to determine germination times in a 'Future Scientist' kit, it measures 2½ x ½ inches. The range is from minus 10° to plus 50°C (15° to 120°F). The glass tube is mounted on a strip of thin aluminium and I hang it in the tent by a safety pin. Although fragile—I put it in the first aid kit for travelling—it gives me much esoteric pleasure. I now know for certain what the night temperature has fallen to when it awakens me. There is no doubt about the temperature of the sea or river if someone shouts "let's swim". With knowledge of the air temperature I can estimate the efficiency of my butane gas stove. I have even made a tiny wet and dry bulb out of it by wrapping the minute bulb in a fragment of water-soaked 'Kleenex' and all sorts of silly things like that.

If thermometers don't turn you on let me commend two home-made items which will save you some cross moments: a dirty pot bag and a windshield for your butane stove. The dirty pot bag is a simple drawstring bag made from lightweight urethane-coated nylon into which goes my fire-blackened canteen. Dirty breakfast dishes too if water has been at a premium. A dirty pot bag prevents soiling to the inside of your packsack and soot on your clothing.

The windshield is also made from urethane-coated nylon—an offcut from tentage I was making. Instead of metal pegs I made two wide tunnel pockets at each end through which I push handy sticks, pointed by my knife. The other two corners are simply forced outwards around the stove by two more pointed sticks. It gets burned once in a while and I then make another one.

My son loathes blowing up an air mattress and devised a clever bellows with a large polybag. He opens up the bag to maximum, gathers it around the filler tube of the mattress and gently squeezes the trapped air into the mattress. It works like a charm. He is a great believer in aluminium kitchen foil. Watch him cook sausages in a little dish of foil over the embers. Builds reflectors for browning dampers too. When there are potatoes around he is a great one for baking them in foil in the firebed. Has designs on cooking fish this way, but somehow we have never got the right sort of fish handy when we have got foil and a good fire.

I am telling you all these trivial little things for one reason. There is so much pleasure to be gained by doing a good improvisation job with materials which lay around. Items which are carried for other functions. Something for nothing, so to speak. Anyone can go into the camp outfitter's store and buy, buy, buy. But it only takes a little ingenuity to do the same thing for virtually no expenditure in money or effort in carrying a thingummyjig which might never be used.

Take the problem with pillows. If you are like me and lie on your side you will like a high pillow to prevent that crick in the neck the following day. But carrying pillows is too big a burden so I tackle it by wrapping all the spare polybottles in my trousers and any spare clothing I have which will not be needed in the night. This bulk completely fills my large stuff sack and despite the nature of the polybottles they present no hard lumps if properly packed.

Packframes and sacks make good backrests for a food stop on the march. Look around for the last few moments before the stop and select a stout stick with a nock in the top. Now prop the pack-frame against this stick at the angle and spread out your pad to sit on and you have a fine high-backed chair. Relax every moment you can. Have five bars of shut-eye at lunchtime if you can manage it.

I should now initiate you into the secret art of making fire without matches. I am told you can do it with a burning glass or a bow fashioned from a piece of your cordage and a whippy stick to twiddle the fire stick at high speed. Careful puffing and lots of twiddling with the bow should generate enough friction for ignition of tinder carried around in an old snuff tin.

The truth is that I can't. Even when I have tried the burning glass routine in high summer all I have raised is a wisp of smoke which has nothing to do with real burning. And I suspect at the time when one needs an emergency light-up there will be no sun around and the kindling will be sodden. Perhaps half a gale will be blowing too.

As for this Archimedes' bow. . . .

So my sincere advice to all lightweighter travellers is to have enough matches for the trip, a further waterproof canister containing a box or so of windproof flamers and deep down in the bottom

Backpacking is for families too. But carrying a child can be very tiring. Try covering less ground instead—there are no prizes for how far you walk

Pots and pans for the lightweight traveller: (*left*) the popular two-man 'Rover' set with an extra one-pint billy; (*top*) a methylated spirit stove which is good for overnight trips in cold weather. All the parts nest together and provide maximum heat recovery from the fuel; (*right*) the 'Wanderer' one-man set developed from the old 'Gilwell' canteen of Scout fame of your pack somewhere a couple of packets of book-matches sealed up in a tiny polybag. If you are a smoker take enough matches to cater for your habit and don't count on your camp supply to see you through. Don't forget to top up the secret hoard after each trip.

I have seen a fascinating little gadget in a Swedish catalogue which I would like to try. It is called a red fire stick and weighs practically nothing. Using a knife it is possible to shave a fat hot spark off the fire stick and keep on doing so "for thousands of lights". Could be a way of lighting up a butane stove when there are no matches left. Could be.

7

Taking your own medicine

There are two sorts of people in this world when it comes to well-being. The blithe and the accident-prone. Only you will know to which group you belong. Before you go travelling light, either on your flat feet, on wheels or in small craft on the water, you must ask yourself this serious question: "Am I accident-prone?" And you had better come up with a truthful answer.

So why are some people blithe? Why can they scoot along like a duck in the water, or thread their way in the hills like mountain goats and yet never come to harm?

I really do not know all the answers, but I have discovered some. For instance, people with imperfect eyesight make errors in spatial judgment and put it down to clumsiness. Others with a defective sense of smell are rarely aware that things are getting hot and wonder why they have small fires and get burns. Loss of hearing often brings with it an uneven sense of balance—especially if the deterioration in audio perception is due to exposure to industrial noise levels of high intensity.

But blithe people are more than just 'normal' people. They are acutely aware of action and consequence—even though they appear to just wander into situations which are fraught with danger. It is necessary, I believe, to always be thinking things through—crossing bridges before you come to them—if one is to stay out of harm's way. Much of this thinking comes with experience, but a great deal is merely common sense.

Commonsense is the backpacker's travelling companion; always at his elbow. Commonsense, which is another way of saying one has thought something all the way through, is so necessary when one goes into the sticks. Commonsense prevents blisters, burns, forest fires, sunburn, drownings, factures, food poisoning, and just about everything else which befalls the human race when it leaves the shelter of its home and familiar daily living.

If commonsense is left behind when going out with a pack on the back trouble will surely fall in step behind. Accidents do not just happen, they are caused.

Even those who take commonsense along can get into trouble when two other conditions are present: hurrying and getting too tired. These deadly twins brush aside prudence and insidiously derange judgment until a situation cannot be thought through properly.

NEVER HURRY. There is plenty of time if you have thought about the trip. If time is running out, stop and make camp before the pressure of the imagined urgency takes charge of your senses. If the rest of the group you are travelling with rushes off ahead and leaves you behind, either cut loose from the group and go it alone at your own pace or tell the leader that the pace is too much. A good leader will slow down at the first sign of too fast a pace for everyone. A bad leader who fails to notice this before distress sets in should not be leading people.

Solo walking puts an extra decision on the man travelling light. He must stop or slow down at the first sign of distress, and the moment when he does so is a matter of fine timing. Swimmy head and blurred vision, stentorian breathing, sweating and uncertain placement of the feet mean that the danger threshold has been passed. To continue is folly.

There should never be cause for hurrying when travelling light. Walking through the big outdoors with a full pack containing a complete life support system on the back ensures that a night halt can be made almost anywhere. Trouble usually comes when a short-cut is being made. But short-cut to where? I thought we went out of doors for pleasure and the heightening of the senses, not an endurance test.

DON'T GET TOO TIRED. Tiredness arises from lack of sleep, lack of food or both. A thermal imbalance in the body's regulator can add another quotient for bad measure.

Tiredness works rather like a drug. It distracts the mind from cause and effect. It promotes mind-blowing ideas for the body to accomplish—ideas which could not be accomplished even when fully rested. It swells pride and prevents a person taking the decision to turn back in bad conditions. Tiredness lures so many people to their deaths.

Rarely should it be necessary to hike for more than eight hours. Rarely should it be necessary to deprive a body of less than eight or nine hours' sleep when out in the sticks. With a properly planned menu list, rarely should it be necessary to be starved of energy—given foods such as sugars and glucose. A shortage of fresh potable water is criminal—never try to economize on the amount you drink.

If you are coming over sleepy, and the sun is still up, pull out the insulating pad, contrive some shade and have a good forty winks. Sleep is the body's natural restorative which should not be ignored.

Now, if you have asked yourself the question I began with, and truthfully you have admitted to yourself that you might be a teeny-weeny bit accident-prone, plan to travel in company. To go solo is only for the blithe and those who are not lonely in their own company.

An ideal group is said to be three, from the point of view of safety. If an accident or an illness arises, there will be one to go and fetch help and another to stay behind as nurse and companion. My experience with threesomes is not entirely successful. Two people seem to dominate the conversation and the interesting jobs to be done leaving the third out in the cold. So work as a twosome or preferably as a four. Then there are natural centres around which the party can revolve with a built-in safety factor.

Most of us are hopelessly inadequate when it comes to real first-aid and dealing with an accident. I do not mean a nicked finger which bleeds a bit or a small burn from the side of a hot pot, I am talking about the real thing: a broken ankle, a compound fracture of the leg, concussion, a severed artery, a drowning or a massive scalding.

Hopefully, if you don't hurry or get too tired and you always think things through, you will enjoy each season of travelling light without so much as a nicked finger. I am convinced that it is possible, and my little first aid kit will take care of these minor troubles if not.

But the big situation could come along. Then what?

ALWAYS LEAVE MEDICAL TREATMENT IN THE HANDS OF THOSE WHO

KNOW HOW TO USE IT. A little first-aid knowledge can be dangerous —never experiment.

So if an accident or major illness occurs, get the fittest in the party to high tail it to the nearest source of help. Telephone first, or go to the doctor's surgery or home. Know the exact location of the injured by Ordnance Survey co-ordinates and await instructions before going back to the injured.

Mountainous areas and pothole districts have an efficient rescue service staffed by skilled volunteers. Other areas are less well covered for emergencies. Take this fact into account when planning a trip.

The man left with the injured party should do no more than reassure, check airways of the injured so breathing can be maintained, and apply pressure with clean clothing to the source of bleeding, and then await the arrival of help. A broken limb should be immobilized to prevent any further damage or extreme pain. Don't try and do more unless you really hold certificates of competence from the St John Ambulance Association.

Of course, drowning is a life and death situation which cannot await the arrival of expert help. I believe everyone should know how to practise mouth-to-mouth resuscitation and the Cornhill Insurance Company, 32 Cornhill, London EC3V 3LJ, will send you a free simple illustrated card to show you how to do it.

Summarized, mouth-to-mouth resuscitation is done this way:

1. Clear the airways. False teeth, a cricked neck, a swallowed tongue, seaweed, dirt.
2. Turn victim on his back, once airways are clear, and move his head backwards as if preparing him to swallow a sword.
3. Wrap a handkerchief around your thumb and hold the jaw open.
4. Pinch nose of victim.
5. Make air-tight contact with your mouth over the mouth of the victim and blow rapidly and forcefully until the victim's chest cage begins to rise.
6. Slip your mouth clear and keeping the victim's mouth open with the bandaged thumb let him exhale the air you have blown in.
7. Repeat the process and try to develop a rhythm about 15 to

20 inhalations a minute. A smooth rhythm is what you are trying to establish even though you will get a bit puffed yourself.

8. Continue until the victim's breathing re-establishes itself or he is obviously dead.

You may have to assist the victim even when he starts breathing again himself. If the fingernails are blue he is not getting enough air.

If you cannot get the rib cage to rise when you blow, there is probably an obstruction in the airway. Double check and get the victim's head right back before you blow again.

If you would like to practise mouth-to-mouth resuscitation, check with your local St John Ambulance organization, which probably holds a training session with plastic mannikins every now and then. They will be delighted to accommodate you.

The other most important knowledge which you must acquire as a lightweighter and know how to deal with is exposure. Exposure, as I outlined in chapter four, is ever-present in the big outdoors and attacks those who are poorly clad, improperly fed, over-tired and out in the open. Exposure is a fast killer unless arrested in time. It can occur even in summer. The chill scale in figure 21 illustrates the relationship of temperature and wind speed.

If you are in a party or alone and some of the following symptoms arise in you or your fellow travellers you must take immediate action:

* Unusual complaints of coldness and tiredness or cramps.
* Deranged mental balance, lethargy and lack of understanding of even simple questions.
* Slurred speech.
* Irrational or violent behaviour. Silly and uncontrollable giggling.
* Abnormal vision.
* Collapse and deep coma.

STOP IMMEDIATELY. Make shelter from whatever is handy. Up tent if it can be done in seconds.

Insulate the patient from any further heat loss—use several sleeping pads under and pile fluffed-up sleeping bags all over. Cover head, face and neck, but leave room for breathing.

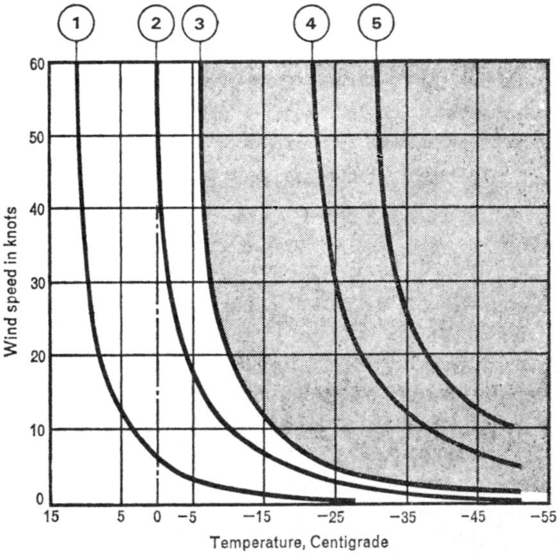

Figure 21. The windchill scale: (1) indicates line when air temperatures feel cold, (2) is bitterly cold, (3) indicates when flesh exposed to the air is liable to freeze and travel becomes unpleasant, (4) is the line of which exposed flesh will freeze within one minute and travel and life in temporary shelters becomes dangerous, (5) shows point when exposed flesh will freeze within half a minute. The shaded area indicates wind/temperature zone which is hostile and dangerous to man's survival.

It can be seen that a man standing in still air at minus 15 degrees Centigrade is no more at risk from exposure than a man similarly clothed standing in a 40-knot wind at plus 10 degrees Centigrade. The message is obvious—if the weather turns very bad, shelter as soon as possible against strong winds, even in summer.

Get the warmest blooded person in the party to lie close with the victim while another makes a warm sugary drink from glucose or Nestlés milk.

Make warm, cheerful, friendly noises to and around the victim to reassure him.

If breathing stops, apply mouth-to-mouth resuscitation as above until normal breathing is re-established.

NEVER RUB THE VICTIM TO RESTORE CIRCULATION
STOP ALL FURTHER EXERTION
NEVER GIVE ALCOHOL

The important object of treating exposure victims is to maintain the body's core heat to prevent failure of vital organs. Once this heat loss is prevented, reversed and external body heat from a companion starts to have effect, the victim should recover equilibrium. Restrain any movement which will cause a further heat loss.

There are some minor afflictions which might bother you on your hike through the big outdoors and I pass on a few simple remedies.

CRAMPS: apply warmth to the afflicted area and do a bit of massage. Dig a bit of salt out of your pack and eat a few grains.

SPRAINED OF TWISTED ANKLE: resist the temptation to remove the boot, it forms an excellent splint. Relief from pain can be obtained by slackening the laces a little. If the boot is removed apply cold compresses and bandage firmly to limit the swelling.

FROSTBITE: hurr with hot breath over the afflicted part until sensation returns. Stick fingers under an armpit or between the crotch. Once the frostbitten part has been rewarmed, keep it warm at all costs. NEVER RUB the parts.

HEAT EXHAUSTION: move over to some shade and swill the patient with cold water or failing this remove a shirt and waft as much cooling air as possible until equilibrium is reached. Rest up for as long as possible.

SUN-BURN: there is no excuse for sun-burn. Never let it happen. Apply Savlon over burned area and get off home.

TOOTHACHE: this is a sign of neglect of dental hygiene. You might have lost a filling. Take an aspirin and crush it with the teeth in the afflicted area. Get home as soon as possible.

DIARRHOEA: a mild attack means laying up with an endless supply of paper and waiting for the attack to subside. Plain boiled rice can help some. Sip a little black tea once in a while. A continuing attack needs medical attention. If you are susceptible to diarrhoea get your doctor to prescribe for you before you begin the trip and take the tablets along as a lucky charm.

CONSTIPATION: it is usual to suffer mild constipation for the first 24 hours of travelling light. The gut is extracting more food value out of your diet than normal and your moisture balance is being disturbed. Normal service should be resumed by the third day. If not, see a chemist.

SNAKE BITE: there is only one poisonous snake in the British Isles and that is the adder or viper. Don't panic, snake bites in Britain are extremely rare and even more rarely cause death—you are more likely to die of fright than venom. Take a couple of aspirin, bandage tightly on the heart side and rest. Send someone to the nearest telephone and call an ambulance. All-over dressing that I have described earlier, will minimize the risk of a deep snake bite. Hiking in shorts in snake country is just asking for trouble. And remember the snake is probably more scared of you than you are of him. Just be sensible in hot weather and watch where you are walking and putting your hands. If you see a snake, treat it as a viper and skirt around it looking where you are going, and not at the snake.

Everyone knows when he feels under par. There is a certain feeling which does not go away as the day develops. Be sensible and take this as a warning sign. Call off the trip and get home if there is still that certain feeling by lunchtime. Better to be ill at home than shivering up in the mountains or deep in a forest. Not only is life no fun for yourself, but it makes everyone else's life a misery too.

Getting lost is no shame. We all do it from time to time. Momentarily anyway. But if you are truly lost, the weather is deteriorating and you are caught out in the wilds, find the nearest sheltered spot, make camp as soon as possible, change into dry things and get some hot food inside you. Next day there should be an improvement in the weather and you will have had time to reconstruct the last stages of your journey on the Ordnance Survey map so that finding yourself again will be no problem. Fear is what you are up against. And this should subside with good hot food and a nice warm sleeping bag. After all, you are well-equipped and self-sufficient. So there is nothing to worrywart about.

If next morning there is only a marginal improvement, pack up slowly and ensure you have a good breakfast inside you. Don't follow streams down water from high hills. Don't take short cuts. Don't try fording rivers. And don't try glissading down a steep-sided hill. Just take it easy and hold your course until you reach a feature which you have discovered on the Ordnance map while you were lying up. Then you can laugh at yourself and join the ranks of those of us who have been lost for a little while.

Summer thunderstorms can be frightening. But it is not the noise that you are risking but the electrical energy. In hills there is a funny eerie prelude to electrical storms. Mountaineers often feel their ice-axes buzzing. Packframes do the same. Nylon clothing gets all crackly. When you experience these signs get off the hills. If there is no prelude and a storm breaks, get off high needles and peaks of hills. Cracks in rocks are good energy pathways—keep well away from them. Don't shelter in caves and overhanging cliffs. You could be struck or walled in from falling rock. Trees in an otherwise open landscape are natural lightning attractors. Keep well away.

It is best to sit or lie down if you are really caught out in a violent thunderstorm. Blow up your air bed if you have one or otherwise sit on your insulating mat and stay put until the storm has rolled away. Chew some chocolate or other sweetmeat, it will help to settle your fear of the great spectacle going on overhead.

If you ever need help, try blowing your whistle. Six blasts with a minute's pause for as long you can. The answer is three blasts followed by a minute's pause and repeated again. At night, flash your torch in the general direction of where help might lie and use the same code: six flashes, followed by a minute's pause.

A small fire covered with damp bracken and grass to make a heavy pother of smoke will also attract attention. Waving the largest piece of international orange material, such as your tent or cagoule, could also raise the alarm.

Conversely, should you ever see or hear these signals yourself, get to the nearest telephone and call for help—don't try and be a hero otherwise you could be another casualty.

As I said at the beginning, always take commonsense with you on the trail. Think things through and be cautious rather than brave. As more and more people take up backpacking there are sure to be some accidents. The Press will love it: "Lone walker in beach rescue drama" or "Camper dies in forest blaze". Can't you just see the headlines? With diligence we can all make sure there are as few such headlines as possible.

8

Travelling Light

Once the lightweight 'bug' bites there is no telling how the fever will break out. It can remain benign and bother a victim only when the weather is fair and the sun high. Or it can return without any real cause like malaria and give a body a shivering fit which eventually ends in a complete rejection of what is being done at the time to be replace by an uncontrollable urge to get off where the skies are big and the wind rustles through the hair. In severe cases it drives the victims to emigrate to far lands in search of large-scale adventure of the sort that cannot be found in Britain with its tiny scales of freedom, fettered by fences, urban development and niggling bylaws.

For those of you that might catch the bug in its most severe form I should like to give you a few tips I've learned during my own bouts of the fever, but for a moment I would like to demonstrate to you how travelling light is not something that is confined to the holidays and week-ends away. Once the knack is learned to plan and manage a backpacker's kit the skills spill over into everyday life and can be of immense benefit whether you are going to Alaska or merely slipping down to the country to see friends for the week-end.

My job has taken me over much of this globe of ours and in common with so many regular jet-setters I have suffered from damaged kit, lost luggage, strikes, mis-routing and even a hijacking attempt. When I first started on world travel I packed in the conventional manner and sat on the lids to get the cases—yes, plural—closed and locked. It took about three miserable journeys and being stranded in Los Angeles while my bags were in Toronto to realize there must be a better way. Lying on my back in California on a king-sized bed with the air-conditioner running full-blast, it came to me. I asked myself why I should have one set of rules for backpacking and another for travelling in 'comfort'. And once I had identified the problem it became a game to see what I could do to modify my kit and still be presentable for meetings in boardrooms or relaxing at the week-end retreat of some company vice-president. Remember that I am a journalist, so I have certain fixed pieces as my stock in trade, such as pencils, ballpoint pens, notebooks, cameras, flash-units, spare film, tape-recorder and spare tapes.

I also move across climatic zones from temperate to tropical to arctic, and very often on the same spell away from my home base. I also go on field visits to rigs out in the desert or platforms offshore and I need special clothing for these too.

I am a classical-music-lover and if there is one thing that lowers my morale it is not being able to listen to, say, the Beethoven C major Quartet, or Rossini's string sonatas, while all around me is the courious atonal music of Arabia or the plaintive and subtle rhythms and dissonances of the Orient. I am not such a phillistine as to pretend there is no other music than that which originates from Europe in the nineteeth century, but after many days of wailing and twanging in taxis, on the hotel radio, in the coffee-shops and the bars, I long for the sonata form of the symphonic mastery of Mahler.

Fortunately for me, technology has come to my aid and since all my music library is now on cassette tape—the same tape that threads in my portable tape-recorder—I allow myself the luxury of perhaps two tapes from that library to find their way into my pack. In Hong Kong, North America and Europe there will be music shops selling high grade pre-recorded tapes and I know I will indulge myself if I find something new, so I limit the travelling music to two tapes from home.

Now I will never pretend that music issuing from the tiny speaker in mono which is fitted to my portable tape-recorder is anything like the beautiful sound coming from my big outfit at home. But I hear the music as it should be played and I can shut out for a while the local brand. I learn about music too—try living with Beethoven's 33 Variations on a Waltz by Diabelli for seven weeks and you too will learn much about composition and execution.

It is perhaps curious that I should place my musical needs first, and yet I find that if the soul is well-nourished anything is possible and the body can put up with a lot of privations. What I was trying to illustrate here is the adaptations that are possible in the needs of the backpacker and the essential requirements of a business traveller. In both cases my tape-recorder is needed. As I hinted elsewhere in the book, I have standardized on one kind of battery —the manganese alkaline AA-sized cell which is available almost anywhere in the world and a spare set has a long shelf life.

Everything electrical that I use while travelling or backpacking is powered by this same type of cell. The flashgun, my faithful Mallory flashlight, by calculator, and my small travelling radio. Only my cameras have a different kind of battery and it is a button-shaped mercury cell which lasts for months.

So having sorted out my needs for the tools of my trade and put the requirements of business travel and backpacking on the same footing I am able to consider the inter-relationship between travelling light for business and pleasure right across the rest of my kit.

International airline regulations regarding passengers make interesting reading. For instance, passengers are allowed to carry into the cabin one bag of not more than 45 by 35 by 20 centimetres or 18 by 14 by 8 inches, for underseat stowage.

The total weight of all baggage including hand luggage is 20 kilos or around 44 pounds. If one reflects that a backpacker's load of 44 pounds is about the maximum for comfort (*see page* 69) then there is no reason at all to pay excess baggage charges when flying.

Airline regulations also allow a passenger to carry on the aircraft a travelling-robe or coat and travelling rug, in addition to a small amount of reading material and a camera or binoculars. This concession for a travelling robe is exploited in the United States by seasoned travellers who buy a zippered robe bag, which is allowable under the rules, and in it goes a suit or two, a spare pair of trousers, a sports jacket, five shirts and in elasticated corner pockets go a pair of shoes.

The robe-bag has all the hooks of the coat-hangers on which the clothes are hung, poking out of the tapered top of the bag and there is a hand-strap at the bottom to facilitate carrying. By folding the bag over and carrying top and bottom together there is no inconvenience. On entering the aircraft—especially if it is an American-made plane—one opens out the robe bag and hangs it on a rail in the wardrobe provided and forgets it for the rest of the flight. On better airlines the steward will bring you the bag as you taxi-in after landing.

It remains for you to decide how best to make use of the maximum size of hand baggage allowed under rules. My own was bought in Kuwait where I did a deal with an Indian merchant after much haggling, and a lot of fun. It is a Samsonite 'Fleebag' and has one main compartment, two full-length side pockets, two small end pockets and an even smaller full-length side pocket. The bag has a broad carrying strap which is adjustable for shoulder length or for use as a hand-strap. The whole is made from tough, soft vinyl material with reinforced corners and a stiffened bottom. Being softly constructed it moulds itself into whatever under-seat stowage space is available, for every airline has a different idea about leg-room and girth allowance. Even in the most tightly spaced internal route airliner I have used I have never once had difficulty in stowing my Fleebag. On lightly loaded planes I often leave it on the seat to the side of me strapped in with the lap belt.

Now this Fleebag has a surprising amount of room and being top zippered is very handy for inflight use. In the main compartment goes my cameras, tape recorder, spare film and tapes—more about this in a moment—toilet kit, sweaters, in-flight slippers and duty free stores. In the larger side pocket goes socks, underwear, T-shirts, ties and other soft items. In the smaller side pocket goes my slim briefcase and a book of crossword puzzles. The end pouches carry my tiny radio, travelling alarm, medical kit, spare batteries, a couple of plastic coinage bags from the bank to hold various bits of small change in the various currencies I will be dealing with. I also stow a few sachets of fresheners every airline so generously provides in the loo.

I took some time to get used to a wrist-purse but travel in Korea and parts of the Middle East soon showed me the value of this useful piece of kit. It must be big enough to carry airline tickets, a passport, traveller's cheques and all the really essential documents one needs. It zips up and the metal tag on the end of the zip passes over the wrist strap for security and the whole is worn on the wrist. A slip pocket on the outside carries the boarding card and a few business cards one so often needs during flight.

Security regulations in some Far Eastern and Middle Eastern

countries are so strict that even my carefully contrived walk-on baggage assembly must be put in the hold. The wrist purse, after minute scrutiny, is finally allowed in the cabin with me. But even the smallest penknife will be taken away before boarding, so I always ensure my trusted knife is in the Fleebag.

As I said earlier, spare and exposed film, tapes and even pocket calculators with memory units are all susceptible to damage from some X-ray baggage screening machines. To obviate this I keep them all in a nylon drawstring bag on top of all my gear in the centre compartment. On passing through security and body-check I remove the bag with the precious film and hand it to the officer and forcibly make him understand that it must not be passed through the X-ray machine. After hand inspection it is handed to the other side for collection after body-check. In that way my precious film is not fogged when my editor asks for my picture spread—it might be useless for other reasons which I won't go into, but not from X-ray fogging!

It is advisable to clear all cameras before boarding and have them ready for inspection and opening. You cannot be too careful in some countries if your pictures are really vital. Don't risk those never-to-be-repeated transparencies by not being prepared.

On my person I wear really comfortable clothes and my boots. Boots can weigh up to six pounds—three kilos—and eat into your baggage allowance as well as being awkward to pack. Time-saving lacing allows one to take boots off in flight and put on travelling slippers in the cabin. Feet swell from long inactivity and reduced air pressure in the cabin so it is not advisable to wear boots all the time.

Wool shirts with two big breast pockets give handy in-flight storage of bits and pieces, and if the toilet bag is stowed on top of the duty-free stores it takes no time at all to get the bag out and freshen up from a long-haul flight.

Since the first edition of this book was published I have grown a beard—purely for practical reasons—and I shall never return to the barbaric practice of shaving. Shaving gear takes up space and increases weight in the kit. Electric razors are always a problem in foreign countries where voltages and plugs are different from our own. Beards, on the other hand, protect the face from sub-zero weather and in the tropics they act as a wick to evaporate sweat rapidly. If you are a shaver there is nothing worse than a thirty-six hour stubble irritating you as you sit tight in some strike-bound airport unable to go and shave for fear of losing your seat among the milling and desperate crowd. Much better to grow a beard properly.

One has to become very self-reliant if one contemplates world travel by air and for this reason I always buy a pound-sized block of Cadbury's fruit and nut chocolate at the airport as emergency rations. The stuff sold at airports is usually suitable for hot climate travel but it is advisable to carry it in a plastic bag to prevent melted chocolate spoiling your kit.

My medical pack is an adaptation of the one in my backpacking kit. I carry 'Lomotil' for relief from an attack of diarrhoea; an anti-histamine cream for minor insect-bites; salt tablets for hot climate de-hydration; water purifying tablets for doubtful water; the usual adhesive plasters; moleskin for protection from chafing; paracetamol pain-killers; a couple of foil-wrapped Alka-Seltzers for hangovers (you tend to get them in my job, from time to time!); a small stick of high-altitude greaseless sunburn and windburn cream; a small dropper bottle of eye-lotion; some mild sleping-tablets such as 'Mogadon' for those occasions when jet-lag prevents proper sleep; scissors and nail-clippers; and a short course of wide band anti-biotics which my doctor prescribes for me and which I renew every six months.

As with backpacking, I regularly review my medical kit and make up the deficiencies, for it is no use being short of some item when you need it badly in the middle of the desert or in a country where pharmacies are so very different from our own and the labels are unfamiliar.

I found a mirror in the cosmetic section of a chain store chemist and that lives in my toilet kit. I have another for backpacking. The mirror is really two circular mirrors that fold in a lightweight plastic frame with a metal hinge. One is plain and the other concave for good magnification to allow one to see grit in the eye. Makes a good shaving mirror if you must shave or trim your beard or moustache.

I am very particular about keeping my international shot record up to date. Vaccination against smallpox is no longer required in many places because the World Health Organization has declared this human scourge is now defeated. But cholera typhoid, typhus, yellow fever, paratyphoid and all the other nasties are still with us. Read the traveller's aid sheets published by the airlines to see what protection you might need that you don't have, and then see your doctor. These consultations are private and you will be required to pay a small fee. However, there is nothing more frustrating than to be turned back at a border or having the job done locally at great expense, so keep an eye on the shot record.

A few years back I was working on an oil rig in Iran at least seventy miles from anywhere. A case of typhoid broke out and a man was flown by helicopter to Shiraz. By the same helicopter returned an Iranian doctor with a Thermos jar full of vaccine. I did not care for his handiwork and to this day I shall never know what he scrawled in my shot record. The moral is: get it done before you leave.

There are tips with clothing too. On one trip I went to Alaska in early spring and within a few days I was in Texas before going to Arizona. It was a long trip that presented many difficulties so far as clothing was concerned. In Alaska I was issued with an enormous goosedown parka and overtrousers as well as down-filled mitts. But around Anchorage I wore my own down-filled sweater under my cagoule and took my wool mitts. I was fine. When I left Alaska I mailed all the cold weather gear back to England and prepared for the heat. Five weeks later I was back home carrying no more than about 25 pounds in my Fleebag and and robe bag.

I have not mentioned raincoats: the reason is I don't use them: instead I pack my rain parka with hood and overtrousers and then I'm prepared for any sort of climate. In Singapore where there is a continuous deluge broken by bouts of hot sunshine—it starts in mid-morning and goes on to sundown—the conventional raincoat is useless. Better to borrow from the backpacker's wardrobe and carry an easily rolled rain parka with hood and overtrousers and the outfit will fold into a slim document case and be available for instant use.

If the rain parka is loose enough, it is possible to wear a down-filled or man-made-fibre-filled sweater under it and then temperate to cold countries are easily catered for. The sweater will compress to a mere handful in a stuffbag and the rain parka, which is only shell clothing, will fold away to almost nothing. Flexibility is what you are aiming for, and while full length cagoules are fine for open country work I believe the zippered rain parka with a press-stud sealed fly-front is a much better garment for the international traveller which can still be used as part of one's backpacking kit.

There is one bonus point in favour of international hotels—for while their international food may be the worst in the world—the laundry service is usually excellent. On some trips I have packed only three shirts—one worn, one clean and one in the laundry—to save weight and bulk. The only problem is that one must stay more than one night in the hotel to hand in the washing before nine in the morning to get the clean stuff back by the same evening.

I always wash out my own smalls and for that reason I carry a small plastic bottle full of liquid detergent suitable for handwashing. The plastic bottles sold on airliners containing Scotch or gin are just fine for detergent, but don't waste the original contents!

Now if the fever gets so bad as to drive you into wanting to go abroad to explore, remember the same rules apply as with international business travel in lightweight style. You want to plan a kit that will allow carry on baggage so that you never need to stand one minute by a baggage carousel awaiting your damaged possessions.

For this reason it is unwise to use big packframes. In North America in the popular hiking districts there are shops which hire all the gear you need including packframes and sacks, tents and even sleeping bags. All you require is a soft rucksack which complies with the size regulations to allow all your essentials to be carried on board and then plan on hiring the rest.

The bulkiest item will be your sleeping bag and cold temperature clothing if you are not seeking the sun. As with international business travel you will be wearing your boots, and there will be no need to carry food—other than emergency rations to cover in-flight delays mentioned previously. Any stove will be banned from baggage anyway for LPG or other hydrocarbon fuels cannot be taken in the air and that includes lighter fuels and aerosols. Better to hire or buy a cheap LPG stove once you have arrived at your trailhead. In North America and Scandinavia there are many well-stocked backpacker's shops which are full of fascinating goodies never seen in Britain—especially AFD foods.

In the United States you will come across the highly prized

Sierra Cup. Buy one for they are useful. The Sierra Cup is a shallow pannikin made of thin stainless steel with a wire handle that tucks under the belt when not being used. On seeing water in the desert you whip out your Sierra Cup pour water over your sun-bleached head and neck before slaking your thirst. You can even brew a cup of coffee or tea directly in your Sierra Cup and I've seen people shave from them—fools! If you hear somebody tell you they had a bath in one, don't laugh because the Sierra Cup is the symbol of backpacking in North America and anything is possible if you have one.

Another useful item is a good sun hat. Look in at a golfing pro-shop and buy one of those deep-peaked golfing hats with an adjustable sweat band. You can dangle a white handkerchief from under the band at the back, Beau Geste-style, and the peak will protect you from glare in the desert or the mountains which is much more powerful than anything we find in Britain. Nothing is more tiring than a blinding headache caused by glare.

As with the business travel medical kit, reform your backpacking kit to take care of local requirements in your selected holiday area. You will hear about snakes that are venemous, such as the rattler and the sidewinder in the United States, and if you are squeamish about such reptiles you will want to buy a snake kit which comprises a rubber tournequet, a scapel blade and a rubber sucker to draw off the venom-loaded blood in the area of the bite. Snake kits are dinky pieces of insurance, but more of a lucky charm than an essential piece of equipment.

Just as dangerous and easily overlooked are scorpions that get in one's boots at night and unsuspecting toes can receive a lethal sting. Always make a habit of banging your boots together when you first rise. Incidently, I know of one authentic case where a man received a scorpion sting and being short of a medical kit slashed the area and applied steak tenderizer. This is not so foolish as it sounds for the tenderizer contains enzymes which gobble up the venom which contains protein and the man lived to tell the tale.

In desert country—the country I love to visit for its majestic beauty—the bugbear is usually the cactus spike. These nasties come in all beautiful forms and you soon learn after brushing past one. The cholla is really ugly for it enters the skin and then the whole joint breaks off, leaving you with a bad problem. The barbs are sheathed and even pulling out the main spike leaves behind a poisonous barb which eventually festers and is very painful. A fine metal comb is one way of deaing with a cholla joint. The better way is to give all cacti plenty of room—there's plenty in the desert.

We British are not very prepared for walking in foreign and hostile vacation spots. In North America everything is very big and help is usually a long way away. The trails might be fairly well marked and the government maps are excellent, but vital things such as finding adequate supplies of water or watching for telltale signs of flash floods when passing through deep canyons are best left to the guiding experts.

An hour or so spent happily in a backpacker's shop inspecting the amazing range of goods available to the Canadian and American packer will almost certainly smoke out a local guide willing to make a four- or five-day trip into the wilderness. He will expect his expenses for food and gasolene to be paid for and the rest will probably be for free since he will almost certainly be an enthusiastic amateur who just loves travelling his local country.

He will teach many tricks; such as where to dig for water in a dry river-bed; where to step to avoid sleeping rattlers; how to read the skies for signs of flash storms; how to read a compass with absolute certainty so that you hit the right trail for an evening halt with plenty of water and fuel for the fire. In American and Canadian wildernesses the large scale maps often have nothing more on them than contour lines and some fancy names like Bumblebee Creek or Dutchman's Canyon. No roads; no houses; no rivers; nothing but wilderness. Then the map and compass take on a new meaning, especially when the midday temperatures can rise to more than 115°F and a false step can mean disaster. . . .

I can feel myself getting the fever again, and that will never do!

* * * * *

The first edition of this book brought one recurring request in letters from so many people; 'Would I describe the ultimate in travelling light?' So for all those who really want to travel like the American Indian, here are a few of my ideas.

As well as a desert walker, I am also a beach walker. The strands of the British Isles are first rate wildernesses and yet the option always exists to drop out and go back to civilization by simply climbing the sea wall or the cliff and catching the first bus back home. Towns festoon our coasts and this means there is always food of some sort around. Except in a few isolated cases where the government still maintains defence zones, beaches are freer of restrictions than any other land in Britain. The sea is always restless and except where people congregate locally, beaches are surprisingly free of other humans. I hope I've made the case for beach walking—especially when I remind you that you don't have to be a mountaineer to do it.

Now a three-day summer walk is just about right for a trial. Choose a place near to you and look at the practicalities; such as trains or buses to get you there, and seaside towns where you can pop in for a meal.

Now tackle it this way—assuming it is settled weather (*see pages* 135 *onwards*). Plan on walking at night when it is coolest and there are fewer people around. Even the most popular beach at midday will be yours at three in the morning as the first light of day is tingeing the sky to the east, or the moon is full, fanning a silver carpet of light across the sea in keeping with your step. The advantage of night walking is a reduction of equipment needed. A full sleeping-bag is redundant, for you sleep in the heat of the day on a half insulating mat—I prefer not to sleep directly on the sand even though it does mould to your contour under the sleeping pad. And trying to find shade for nothing is worse than sleeping in direct sun.

If it should rain, ensure you have a big cape with a hood under which you can crawl. The cape will protect you during your walking and become your bivouac when you are resting.

Plan on there being some cool winds, either at night or during the day when you are sleeping. An anorak with a light quilting of man-made insulation will be adequate as a sleeping-bag top during the day and beating the cool wind at night. Make sure the anorak has lots of pockets for bits and pieces: matches, string, compass (if you like playing with them), tide-table (*see page* 131), fresheners, paper handkerchiefs, comb, toothbrush, insect repellent, sweet meats, mints to kill the salty taste in the mouth from hard walking, lip salve to stop drying from wind, sun-glasses; a strip of Ordnance Survey map cut out and pasted on durable material will add to your enjoyment; and all these things will stow in your anorak.

I have a rally jacket I use which is ideal. It has a lightweight hood that stows inside the collar for days when the wind bites or the sand is blowing. It has zippered inside pockets, a couple of breast pockets with poppers on, a double-ended main zip, and two side pockets as well as an arm pocket to carry small items.

My trousers are golfers' lightweight twill, cut full and almost windproof, yet lightweight. I wear a T-shirt and carry one spare, and in the waist pack, which I will describe in a moment, I carry a light woollen sweater with sleeves. I also carry a spare pair of socks and spare underwear. If you like swimming you will need a pair of swimming-trunks too. I prefer to go in in the buff early and clean off the travel sweat before finding a place to curl up. I also carry a terry towel flannel which I use as a mini-towel. A rub over with this and several wringings soon gets you dry in the summer, even before the sun is properly up. It will dry out as you sleep.

I take no food, except for some raisins and peanuts, planning on eating in some seaside café or boarding-house, pub or hotel. Short-order food is always around in a seaside town. Try the station buffet if all else fails!

But I do take a belt-mounted water-bottle into which I mix a citrus-based fruit drink powder for a thirst-slaker. I wear lightweight boots and always have short gaiters to stop pebbles finding their way in.

Now when I first started I carried a haversack but now I have a waist sack which belts around my lower trunk. With stuff stowed in my anorak I hardly need all the space it provides. The water-bottle fits on the belt and I'm in business: self sufficient, with the exception of food and water.

My day goes like this. I plan on walking from around ten at night until four or five the next morning, having first studied what lies ahead of me on the map. Then I quit at some suitable spot on the edge of the town, nibble some sweetmeat, have a bathe in the sea before unrolling my slip of a mat and settling down for an hour or so. The sun usually wakens me around nine and then I set off to find breakfast and a look around the town. Then I walk on a little further and find another resting spot for the afternoon. Hunger will awaken me late in the afternoon and then I find some supper, perhaps a pint or two, and take to the beach again. I can recommend the idea to you, and if the weather really turns out foul, quit and catch a bus back home.

9

A means to an end

So here we are, all dressed up, somewhere to go and yet nothing in mind. We have spent some hard-earned cash, had a couple of weekends away, found to our delight that backpacking is not roughing it nor is it very tough on the constitution. Quite the reverse, in fact.

Now I can amble along quite aimlessly, with nothing in mind but the view. I must confess there are times when I travel with a purpose, but that is not my usual wont. More often than not I go solo to get some respite from the pressure of my daily craft. Instead of thinking about deadlines, interviews, printers and publishers, I consume my thinking time with the simple pleasures of cooking a good meal or dozing through a rainstorm to the music of the raindrops hammering on the taut flysheet. I pride myself that I have a good sense of smell and I put it to work on the trail sniffing the scented air of the woodland and hedgerow. I sniff the evening air after rain as a badger would at dusk as he emerges from his den. A shower of rain is good for clearing up the jumbled smells accumulated during the heat of the day and laying them out fresh again layer by layer. With a keen nose you can get quite distinct and separate drifts of scent. There is the overall background smell of the forest bed—a dank decaying sort of smell. Clothing this layer might be a steady drift of pine resin oozing under the filaments of the bark. Then like jewels come the little snatches of hedgerow flowers and herbs, ranging from heady delight to sharp astringency.

Even the washed air has a different smell—a sort of sweet odour of a coke brazier, sharp and bracing. By the canal-side there is a smell I can only describe as a brown-paper scent—except in the lock chambers when the smell turns sweet and 'green'.

But this sort of reverie is not travelling light with a purpose. It is purely an indulgence—a convalescence from the stink of diesel and bad street drains; stale beer stench drifting from a street-side pub or overcooked onions and denatured beef patted into sacrificial burgers; newsprint and ink; underground trains and exhaled tobacco smoke; other people's sweat and other people's aftershave. Ugh!

So if you must have a purpose in life; a secret attic in the mind into which you can withdraw to open the dusty hampers of memory and examine the treasures collected over a lifetime, let me offer a few suggestions that travelling light can enhance.

Take what my son has done for me. At a tiny age—I suppose it was because he was so much closer to the ground than I—he began taking a long look at insects. Up until this time I always swatted, squashed or trod on anything that crawled, buzzed, wriggled, and hovered. I suppose all creepy crawly things are a mild threat to most people and to some a source of horror. My son changed all this. Bit by bit he handled with delight the things that crawled, buzzed, wriggled and hovered and held them up to me for close inspection. Under the eyeglass and enlightened by the recitation of his patient researches I began to have less fear of the insect kingdom and later stood in awe at its complexity and enormity. Goodness knows there are too many people on this planet, but the mind boggles at the thought that over 600,000 insect *species* have so far been identified and some authorities suggest that this might be only about ten per cent of all the insect species yet to be discovered. The frequency in each species outnumbers man many thousands of times to one.

Because of this extreme range of species, there is plenty of room for the serious amateur insect observer or entomologist. Entomology fits in well with travelling light because the size and weight of the quarry is in scale with the craft. The kit necessary for the hobby is equally unsophisticated and light to carry—nor is it very bulky.

Most of us have collected some strange insect in a matchbox and taken it home for identification. This is a good start. You can add a good watchmaker's eyeglass of about four diopters, a small glass bottle with a gas-tight screw lid in which has been stuffed some toilet paper and a perforated cardboard disc. This bottle makes a good field killing bottle when used in conjunction with a little carbon tetrachloride. Add a pair of tweezers, a small cigar box lined with corrugated cardboard, a penny notebook for field notes, a lightweight butterfly net of about two foot diameter and three foot long cone kept open by a light hoop of spring stainless steel wire and a couple of small 'Jubilee' clips to mount the net on a handy sapling cut from the hedgerow, and a smaller, heavier net with folding aluminium rod yoke for sweeping along grasses and hedge bottom vegetation and you are in business.

Paul Hamlyn publishes some good introductory coloured booklets on insects and natural history collecting which should start you off in the right direction. These books weigh only about six ounces and will bring you hours of fascinating pleasure as you begin to explore into the insect kingdom. Bit by bit you will accurately be able to identify the creatures that share your lightweight world with you and less and less will your boot blindly obliterate them as you understand their complex life cycles and habits. Only ignorance brings imagined threat: knowledge is a revelation.

Many times my son and I have spent hours of intense observation when we would otherwise be walking blindly down the trail. Maybe we did not cover more than a dozen miles in a weekend—but so what? We both learned a lot—especially I.

Examination of pond life is a natural extension of insect collecting but it does have the penalty of heavier gear and the weight of carried water in which specimens are brought home for further study. Even so, pond life observing is very rewarding and a natural link in the understanding of the world around us that we threaten by our careless, avaricious and thoughtless human existence. It is only when you begin to dip litmus papers into idyllic-looking streams and discover the awfulness of pollution and the breakdown in the long ecological chain—which includes us humans—does the desperateness of the situation become apparent.

If there is one thing I have learned from the young it is the awareness of the dreadful mess which we are about to bequeath them in a few decades. Moreover, I have discovered this impending disaster by travelling light with my eyes open.

Talking of keeping eyes open—the first things that an urban dweller sees, when he ventures forth into the country with a pack on his back, are unfamiliar birds. Bird watching needs the minimum of equipment when travelling light. Even a good pair of eyes will do, but a lightweight monocular or a specially made pair of binoculars weighing perhaps twelve ounces, bring the wonderful world of birds into full view. The only other piece of equipment necessary is a small field identification book and perhaps a penny notebook for recording notes.

Birds, thank goodness, are still fairly plentiful in the spaces that man has not yet fouled too much. Of course, hawks, warblers, marsh birds, estuarial birds and smaller passerines are threatened everywhere—especially during migration. Some species we might never see again, others only very rarely where once they flourished.

Just the other day—it is winter as I write—I went down onto the marshes and walked all one day trying to straighten out thoughts for this book. My boots scrunched into the frosted sand at the tide edge and far out on the mud where the scum was oozing back with the flood were hundreds of oyster catchers feeding up ready for the next stage of their migration towards the sun.

Soon there came literally thousands of curlews scampering on dithery wings over my head as they dropped into the water-meadows just over the sea wall. I have never seen so many down-turned bills and heard so many trilling pipes.

But the biggest surprise was yet to come. Almost at my feet and without any show of fear by my presence were little birds with white breasts, brown wings and stubby beaks. They trotted here, there and everywhere, rising every now and then to fly forward. The splash of white as they rose gave them away in the dusken light—snow buntings. Dozens and dozens of them. And I was sentimentally glad to be among this threatened branch of warm-blooded life. Here was I, alone with no other human within a mile or so of me, on a drear winter afternoon. I was clad in my usual rig of boots, two pairs of socks, tights and woollen trousers, string vest, cotton T-shirt, woollen sweater, woollen shirt, down jacket, cagoule, scarf and woollen mitts—sucking Kendal Mint Cake and still feeling the raw wind on my cheeks, while all about me were hundreds of tiny birds wearing only what they had stood up in since they left Scandinavia some days before. If the marshes were good to them they would find enough juicy, chilly grubs and worms to live to fly another day—another day further south. I felt quite humble in my technologically-based comfort.

But all around me was cause for anger. Plastic rubbish discharged heedlessly by passing ships was matted into the tide edge. And worse. There for those with eyes willing to see such things was the deadly calling card of our industrialized world—the oil slick. The samphire on the salting's edge was smothered and it clung to the lugs of my boots, black, vile and uncompromising. How many more winters will the snow-bunting come to my marshes? How many more winters will it find succour in the desolate landscape that only fools like me share with the birds?

Earlier this year I was walking in a Derbyshire dale. A sheer limestone cliff towered over me. At the top were overhanging trees and down to the left ran a trout stream. There were tree creepers and nuthatches flashing in the waterside thicket, but high overhead there was a hawk.

Until you have seen a hawk in its natural habitat, in my opinion, you have not lived. This hawk kept launching off into the up-going current of warm air and fidgeting the ends of its primary feathers, adjusting its eagle-spread tail and watching me, first with one eye and then the other. We played a game, that hawk and I. I pretended not to watch him and ambled slowly up the dale. He, not fooled by this ploy, followed me in little agitated sidles until I had left his patch, then in a majestic display of aerial mastery he swooped back down the dale and landed to preen himself in the late afternoon sun.

About a mile away from this dale there are grouse moors where rich sporting men and their loaders bring their luncheon hampers and matched Purdie guns. I wonder if my noble hawk has survived the 'glorious fourth'?

The thing about watching birds when backpacking is the sense of perspective it gives to the slenderness of life.

If the future of the living is too much for you when tramping around the countryside, why not turn to a death that happened millions of years ago and marvel in the abstract. Another of my son's hobby horses is fossil hunting.

Of course we are fortunate in our little part of Suffolk—we stand on Red Crag—a kind of earth laid down by the sea in the Upper Tertiary and the Pleistocene periods over five million years ago. Every now and then this crag becomes exposed at the surface and this is the happy hunting ground of the fossil collector. Specimens are mostly shells, sharks' teeth and corals, but crab pincers and even mammalian teeth are to be found.

Fossils occur in a wide distribution throughout Britain. Even old coal tips can provide specimens which have been dug out of the mine and because they were formed in the useless shale have been discarded. In the limestones of Derbyshire and the cliffs of Dorset there are rich finds including the wonderful ammonites. Railway embankments and canal cuttings can be rewarding too.

Fossils often bear a rich natural polish of their own which has withstood millions of years of time. Mounted on a wooden panel and hung on the wall, fossils make a unique decoration in the home as well as being of scientific interest.

Equipment for fossil hunting is quite simple. You will need a trowel—a bricklayer's pointing trowel will do—a wide sable hair brush, a sieve made from a household plastic flour sieve, and when you are among rock a small chisel and a geologist's hammer are an advantage. The hammer could be dispensed with and a handy stone used instead—but watch out for blood blisters from crushed fingers.

Specimens can be conveyed in a plastic box similar to a food box which has been stuffed with cotton wadding to prevent the fossils banging together and becoming damaged. A small optical eye glass of four diopters will help to examine tiny fossils found in alluvial sands and crag. As with most other collecting hobbies, a small field notebook to record the site and date of find is essential.

The department of palaeontology at the British Museum publishes some very cheap but infinitely valuable field and reference books to help fossil collectors. The line drawings are extremely accurate and works of art in their own right.

From fossils to rock and mineral collection is but a short step and needs no special field equipment other than a geologist's hammer and a chisel. A collecting bag for specimens helps to keep the stones together and the packsack becoming loaded with dust and grit. Collecting rocks which will polish, either in a tumble polisher or by hand on a piece of plate glass with water and various grades of abrasive, is an absorbing hobby which is fast becoming a fad. Beautiful stones abound—especially on beaches—and there are many semi-previous stones to be picked up right under your feet when you go over wild beaches. Our East Anglian beaches are famous for ambers and carnelians which can be polished to jewel-like quality. Even agates make good jewellery, so it is possible that your rock collecting might even help pay for your new tent or that expensive winter sleeping bag.

Metallic ores and minerals often occur in the natural state in the most exquisite shapes and colours. Pyrites and copper nodules need no further treatment after selection before mounting. Calcites and zincites are equally attractive. The quest for minerals will take you to some of the rarest and most beautiful parts of our national heritage, and will also make you well aware of the damage commercial prospectors can do to the landscape if they are thoughtlessly granted planning permission to mine in areas of outstanding natural beauty.

As I have mentioned elsewhere, my own travelling is on beaches. It suits my mood and my energies yet takes me away from people in a trice. It also brings me in contact with the wonderful ecology of the littoral—that vague area between the shallow waters of low tide and the threshold of farmland where it meets the beach.

Not unnaturally then, I have become interested in conchology—the study of shells. These fascinating creatures of the tide edge and sand bar have evolved but little since the time of the specimens which my son finds as fossils. Even the Latin names are similar and one can move from one discipline to the other with ease once the conchology bug bites you.

Shells occur everywhere, but not all species are available on every beach. The big razors of the Barmouth estuary are not found among the horse mussels of the Wash. The chitons of the Gower peninsula do not occur among the winkle beds of Essex.

Many of the living shellfish make good eating too, so if you are travelling light and find cockles or oysters you have found a food bonus.

Shell hunting needs no special equipment—only a practised eye for blow holes and a sharp stick with which to go digging. Shells are quite light to carry so even a good haul does not add too much weight to the total load to be carried. But some shells are extremely fragile so wrap them well if you do not want to be disappointed by the time you arrive home.

Stella Turk's book *Collecting Shells* (Foyles) will give you a good start. The Young Specialist series booklet *Seashore* by Kosch, Fierling and Janus will not only help you with shells but all manner of creatures, on, in and by the sea. This booklet weighs 8 ounces and would make a good packfriend if you have weight to spare.

I know nothing about botany—I wish I did. I know even less about trees, except to identify the right ones for firewood. Perhaps one of these days I shall get around to hunting wild flowers and things like that, but I do not think I shall have much time this side of my 80th birthday.

One bug I have got out of my system, photography, was cured by being a professional. A professional has to have a camera which consistently gives the optimum results under all lighting conditions and go on working in weather which would cause an amateur to put his treasured camera away for fear of damage. The professional finds one developer which suits him and sticks with it. He uses only two or three colour emulsions and generally only one black and white. This way he can achieve consistent results which will sell. It is practical viewpoint the amateur refuses to see.

Of course professionals have fashions and fads—Nikon this year, Hasselblad last, Rolleiflex a decade ago. But the fashion changes only because there is a definite gain with each new marque. Reliability is always the criterion—gadgetry comes last.

So if you are keen on photography and want to travel light with your camera think about what you want from your photography before you spend a lot of good money. For instance, and I am assuming you are a serious worker, your choice of format will either be 6×6 or 35 mm. Remember, if you hope to sell your pictures later, a good big 'un beats a good little 'un any day.

Most art editors like Kodachrome II colour stock for 35 mm if they can get it. You might get away with Agfa CT 18 but only if the pictures are unique. I doubt if any other emulsions will pass the light table of an art editor's desk. For colour stock on 6×6 format, the most commonly used colour is Kodak Ektachchrome Professional and Ektachrome High Speed when the light is too poor. Transparencies are preferable to colour prints.

As for black and white emulsions, most professionals use either Kodak Tri-X or Ilford FP4 and HP4. Development is in either D-76 or ID-11. Most professional printing for reproduction is done on Kodak Press F single weight. The most acceptable print size is 10×8 or whole plate—nothing smaller. Every picture or transparency must be captioned clearly and simply in a few words.

In another chapter I mentioned the half-frame format for mono photography and I still believe the Olympus Pen system is good for the serious amateur who travels light. Recently I have taken to the full-frame Olympus cameras, such as the Trip 35, if I think

I might just lose my camera in bad conditions; or the 35 ED which does all my thinking for me and I come home with a high percentage of properly exposed shots.

For 6×6 work the old-fashioned Rolleiflex T still soldiers on being good for both colour and mono work despite its limitations. The main drawback is that it weighs 3 pounds 2 ounces.

If you are intending to travel light in vile weather, sea spray and driving fine dust you might like to look at the Nikkonos waterproof 35 mm camera. Although it has restrictions of aperture and speed, its semi-wide angle lens is good and I can testify to its efficiency in bad environments.

The biggest mistake most amateurs make when photographing a landscape in colour is to make the exposure in flat overhead lighting. Try and work before nine in the morning and after five in the evening in summer when shadows are long and there is warmth in the colour. Experiment with against the light colour work and heavy mist backgrounds—even pouring rain if you have a bit of your bright red kit in the foreground. Try and make each picture tell only one story—two story pictures distract the viewer. Get some red and blue colour correction filters to change the mood of the overall chroma of the picture and kill the bright greens of foreground grass areas.

A polarizing filter will give good intensified blue skies at right angles to the sun on clear bright days. Autumn and spring are good times for colour-workers. Snow is tricky but very rewarding especially up-light. If you are travelling solo and want to record yourself in the picture make sure your camera has a 15-second delay on the shutter or carry a delay mechanism so that you can get in the picture to make it interesting.

A piece of nylon cord stretched from under the boot to a socket screwed into the tripod bushing steadies the shakes for very little extra weight. For macro-photography a small universal head and clamp is ideal, and extension tubes weigh very little.

Of course most serious amateur photographers will not need me to tell them what to do and what not to do. Each to his own last. But if you are not a serious worker and look upon photography only as a record in a snapshot of your travels, choose a simple and reliable camera which has few gadgets on it and 'thinks' out the shutter speeds and apertures for itself. Then you can concentrate on the picture and not on the camera. The results, when they come back from the processors will let you relive the moments when you travelled light and found a new dimension to your life—and surely that is what most photography is all about?

I have not exhausted all the things your lightweight travelling can do to further your hobby. For instance, I sometimes take a small tape recorder along with me to capture some dialect which is in danger of dying out as the mid-Atlantic accent swamps Britain. I could easily be taping bird songs or building up a 'word book' dictated to the recorder as I happen along.

Just remember the ounces, that's all. A bit here and a bit there soon adds up to a heck of a lot and you could end up with more weight carried for your hobby than the essentials for backpacking in comfort. But that is your affair.

10
A winter's tale

Life is somewhat like a living tide, spaced by the period of the sun rather than the feckless diurnal swill of the ocean which only obeys the pull of the moon.

In high summer we froth over the upper rim of our personal strand driven by the fresh winds of our ambitions. In deep winter we quietly drain to the far edge of our consciousness and hopefully wait for the tide to turn again.

Today, Boxing Day, was for me the moment the tide turned. Across the blue-grey marshes the sun subsided into the marram grass horizon and a brown froth-edged nuzzle of a new tide dribbled up the gulleys between the saltings. One moment, all around had been plated in 21-carat gold. The next, the world turned to pewter. It was incredibly mild.

A zephyr of wind from the south-west reeked of iodine sweated by the drying bladderwrack. Under my boots lay a carpet of shells—their owners eaten long ago by the restless waders. Cockles, periwinkles, oysters and mussels by the million. My passing crunched noisily and raised clouds of cirl buntings from the lifeless stalks of the Norfolk reeds in the nearby delph.

As far as I know, I was alone on the marshes. The last humans I had seen had eyed me cautiously in the lane, hours before. While the sun was still high a small boat had buzzed by on the far side of the river taking a couple of fishermen home with their catch. They shouted to each other above the din of the outboard and their every word carried across the freckled water towards me—that's how I know they had a catch.

I happened upon a clear water pool. Dammed in by nodules of clay. The bottom of the mirrored liquid was alive with shrimp-like creatures dashing in a mad frenzy at the first slant of my shadow until only tiny clouds of silt showed where they had all plunged head first from my gaze.

Then there came the Brent geese. About fifteen of them. Noisy, clumsy, deliberate and hungry. They waddled towards the edge of the saltings in a ragged line, black necks crooked low over their feeding. Grunting. But the look-out saw me. His sombre head erect and bill turned over his plump shoulders he waited a moment to be sure I was a real threat, then gave the signal. The grunting stopped and without question the gaggle waddled into the end of the creek. There was a mighty beating of wings and treading of webbed feet. Necks outstretched the geese wound themselves into the air and turned into the sun and were lost to me.

In the quiet after the geese had flighted I began to dream of next year. Of blue wood smoke rising vertically for a hundred feet to flatten and blanket beyond my camp on the still summer evening air. And the first skin of dew spread on the orange canvas. Coffee fragrance mingling with the acrid plume rising from my fire. Tiredness, tingling feet, a full belly staunched with curry, bats zipping low overhead, stars like holes punctured in a velvet curtain. Too good to leave—too late to stay awake. . . .

In another reverie I was high up somewhere. The windward side of the tent roof was bellied inwards towards me in the dim early morning light. A summer gale was racing over the brow of the low and roaring like a drunken fool down the hillside towards me. Blundering, blustering, hammering at the stone hedge, rasping through the trees in the copse below. And just as drunkenness brings unpredictable behaviour, there was a strange moment's silence before the next onslaught.

The rain came like showers of hard rice at a wedding party, but in gigantic handfuls. I feared a little for the security of the pegs I had driven so carelessly the night before. And what of the stuff I had left outside? I fumbled for the torch in my boot. Blinked, owl-like, in the brilliant light funnelled over my wrist.

Ten minutes, the finger stood, before the hour of three.

For hours and hours I dangled between sleep and panic as the gale shrieked itself into a storm. Inside the snugness of the sleeping bag I felt only half secure yet strangely remote from what was going on outside. Then I dozed more securely, to awaken in the brilliant burning glass light of sunshine dazzling through the thin membrane of nylon which, miraculously, was still standing. All was quiet. Did I dream? Whatever did I eat for supper last night?

But ripping back the zip-fastener revealed the morning, scrubbed and washed by the night's storm. The sky was the shade of long-washed jeans. Scudding across this opalesque morning were slate-grey cloudlets ragged and rouged underneath in the wet morning sun. My son's tent stood nearby, intact and glistening. The door zips opened and a tangled head slowly emerged tortoise-like from under the green carapace of canvas.

"Quite a storm," he said, running his fingers through his hair and yawning wide. It was my turn to make the morning tea. . . .

The crunch of shells under my boots gives way to the soft thud of feet on hardening clay. I am in the lane again as darkness falls. An owl tunes up for the night's adventures in the spinney. Rain pools fringed at the edge by horse's hoofprints reflect a gibbous moon hanging far out over the sea. Only a magenta afterglow remembers how good this glorious Boxing Day has been. At home the manuscript for this book lies in its crib of well-thumbed folders, born now. A separate thing which I have carried these last nine months. Nothing I could do now—save destruction—will change it.

Nor do I want to change it. If I remember all those months ago when *The Backpacker's Handbook* was just a twinkle in my eye, did I see things so much differently? It is no clever thing that I and thousands of travellers do when we collect the products of manufactory around us and plan a journey. The assembly of a backpacker's kit is a process of trial and error; acceptance and rejection according to fancy or fancied need. It is the reality of using the kit which suggests changes in what is, after all, only a roof, a bed and a pantry for all seasons.

What really matters, my friend, is how you personally use the many pieces and ideas which I have gathered together in this book. Accept them, reject them, do as you wish with them. But above all travel light and enjoy the outdoors in whatever form suggests itself to you. And when you have seen for yourself at close quarters the mounting pressure on the natural world be prepared to defend it whenever the need arises.

In this way, should the world last that long, our children's children will still be able to travel light and glimpse a little of what we have enjoyed.

Appendix I

USEFUL ADDRESSES FOR FURTHER INFORMATION

TENTS

Camp Trails: 4111 West Clarendon Avenue, Phoenix, Arizona 85019, USA.

Camp Trails International, Waterford Industrial Estate, Waterford, Ireland.

Robert Saunders: Desiree House, Five Oaks Lane, Chigwell, Essex.

Ultimate Equipment: Warkworth, Morpeth, Northumberland.

PACK FRAMES

Brown Best: 47 Old Woolwich Road, London SE10.

Karrimor: Weathertite Products, Avenue Parade, Accrington, Lancs.

SeAb: Banton Limited, Meadow Lane, Nottingham.

SLEEPING BAGS AND DUVET CLOTHING

Black and Edginton: Port Glasgow, Scotland.

Point Five: Banton Limited, Meadow Lane, Nottingham.

Polywarm Products: PTC-Langdon Limited, Curtis Road, Dorking, Surrey.

Mountain Equipment, George Street, Glossop, Derbyshire.

MAJOR OUTFITTERS

Black and Edginton: Port Glasgow, Scotland, and Ruxley Corner, Sidcup, Kent.

Robert Lawrie: 54 Seymour Street, London W1H 5WE.

Pindisports: 14–18 Holborn, London EC1, and provincial branches.

The Scout Shop: Churchill Industrial Estate, Lancing, Sussex, and at branches in most large towns.

Youth Hostels Association Services: 14 Southampton Street, London WC2; also 35 Cannon Street, Birmingham B2 5EE, and 36 Fountain Street, Manchester M2 2BE.

TENT PEGS AND POLES

The Hampton Works (Stampings) Limited: Twyning Road, Stirchley, Birmingham B30 2XZ.

ASSOCIATIONS AND CLUBS

Canoeing Club of Great Britain and Ireland: 11 Lower Grosvenor Place, London SW1.

Central Council for Physical Recreations: 70 Brompton Road, London SW3.

The Countryside Commission, John Dower House, Crescent Place, Cheltenham, Gloucestershire.

Ramblers' Association, 1–4 Crawford Mews, York Street, London W1.

British Canoe Union: 26–29 Park Crescent, London W1.

Mountaineering Associations: 102a Westbourne Grove, London W2.

Scottish YHA: 7 Bruntsfield Crescent, Edinburgh 10.

Youth Hostels Association: Trevelyan House, 8 St Stephen's Hill, St Albans, Herts.

The Backpacker's Club: Eric Gurney, 20 St. Michael's Road, Tilehurst, Reading.

Appendix II

USEFUL BOOKS

HISTORICAL

Kephart, Horace, *Camping and Woodcraft*; Macmillan N.Y., 1967.

INSPIRATIONAL

Fletcher, Colin, *The Thousand-mile Summer*; Howell-North, California, 1963.

Fletcher, Colin, *The Man who Walked through Time*; Alfred A. Knopf, 1967.

Hemery, Eric, *Wilderness Camping in Britain*; Robert Hale, 1970.

Hillaby, John, *Journey through Britain*; Constable, 1968.

Hillaby, John, *Journey through Europe*; Constable, 1972.

INSTRUCTIONAL

Blackshaw, Alan, *Mountaineering*; Penguin, 1965.

Blandford, Percy, *Tackle Canoeing this way*; Stanley Paul, 1969.

Frankel, L & G, *Bike-ways*; Oak Tree Press, 1971.

Jackson, John, *Safety on Mountains*; Central Council Physical Recreation, 1968.

Pyatt, Edward, *Coastal Paths of the South West*; David and Charles, 1971.

DIRECTIONAL

British Museum, *British Caenozoic Fossils*; Trustees of the British Museum (Natural History), 1968.

Bruun, Bertel, *Birdwatching*; Hamlyn, 1967.

Clegg, John, *Pond Life*; Frederick Warne, 1967.

Fisher, James, *Shell Nature-lovers' Guide*; Rainbird, 1966.

Hahnewald and Hutchinson, *Wild Flowers in Colour*; Penguin, 1958.

Harris, Reg, *Natural History Collecting*; Hamlyn, 1969.
Kosch, Frieling and Janus, *Seashore*; Burke, 1963.
Riley, Norman, *Insects in Colour*; Blandford, 1963.
Turk, Stella, *Shell collecting*; Foyle, 1966.
Vedel and Lange, *Trees and Bushes in Wood and Hedgerow*; Methuen, 1962.

Appendix III

STOVE EFFICIENCY

There are many stoves available to the lightweight traveller and it is not easy to choose the right model. In a series of controlled tests I took six popular models; two petrol, one paraffin, two butane and one alcohol, and deduced their *rated* efficiency.

For instance, all stoves were made to boil one pint of 50°F water at sea level with a barometric pressure of 30·00 inches in an ambient temperature of 70°F and the time noted. Then each stove was filled to maximum and burned right out. Then all the other stoves were rated against the longest burning stove to find the true *carried* weight. For instance, the longest burning stove was the Camping Gaz Bleuet S200 which weighed only 18 ounces. The SVEA 123, although only weighing the same amount as the S200, burned out completely in 45 minutes. To achieve the same burning time as the S200 extra fuel had to be carried in metal cans of high integrity—the petrol fuel cannot be transported in polybottles—and when the all-up weight was measured the SVEA 123 was found to be 44 ounces as compared with the S200 at 27 ounces.

Of course butane stoves lose their efficiency as the temperature drops. At freezing they hardly worked at all while the petrol and paraffin stoves showed little fall in efficiency. From the rated tests I would recommend butane stoves for summer travel in Britain and the Continent and the Primus 96 for general all year round back-packing—despite the extra weight penalty and the reek of spilled paraffin should it get into the kit.

All the tests were run at full throttle in still air. The boiling times increase considerably in wind and with altitude.

Model Type	Wt. empty (oz.)	Wt. full (oz.)	Boiling time (see text)	Charge (oz.)	One charge burning time	Fuel type	Rated weight (see text)	Stability 0–5
SVEA 123	18	22	3 m 30 s	5½ fl/oz.	45 m	Petrol	**44** oz.	3
OPTIMUS 8R	26	29	5 m 30 s	4½ fl/oz.	45 m	Petrol	**50** oz.	5
PRIMUS 96	28	35	5 m 10 s	9 fl/oz.	140 m	Paraffin /meths	**40** oz.	4
TILLEY GO-GAS	17	25	5 m 35 s	6 oz.	175 m	Butane	**33** oz.	3
BLEUET S200	18	27	4 m 35 s	6¾ oz.	195 m	Butane	**27** oz.	4
SeAb Stormcooker	31†	35	5 m 45 s (when warm)	5 fl/oz.	50 m	Alcohol	**55** oz.	3

† Includes weight of integral cooking pots.

Index